Engraved by J.C. Buttre.

MARY L. DAY.

INCIDENTS

IN THE

LIFE OF A BLIND GIRL.

MARY L. DAY,

A Graduate of the Maryland Institution for the Blind.

BALTIMORE:
PUBLISHED BY JAMES YOUNG,
114 WEST BALTIMORE STREET.

PREFACE.

IN offering this little volume to the public, and soliciting for it countenance and patronage, it may be fitting to state, the incidents narrated are facts simply given, with no over-wrought coloring of fancy. The design, in its issue, is one highly commendable to its author—a laudable desire to obtain a livelihood independent of those kind friends who fain would render personal effort, in this respect, quite unnecessary.

The beneficent can but favor such an effort, and tender the most practical approval. Unto those whom God has seen fit to afflict, is it not our duty to lend a helping hand? They are travelling earth's beaten paths, as are we; if obscured the sun, shall we not drive away the mists by kindly word or cheering smile?

Of the numerous dispensations it is our lot to bear, that of blindness seems, indeed, the most severe—the helplessness and dependence it induces should appeal to every heart. It is true, orbs of vision closed on light of sun or moon, the more may celestial light shine inward; yet, to tread Earth's garden-paths, forever veiled the beauty of sky or flower, is a heavy cross to bear. There are avenues of happiness which afford intense enjoyment, forever closed to the unfortunate who can not see the greatness of God in tinting the violet's velvet lining, or in the delicate rose-leaf's mystic loveliness—who may not gaze on his goodness in arching the heavens with the beautiful covenant bow, or in spreading the earth with a soil yielding, in unbounded luxuriance, herb, tree, fruit, and flower.

Wishing the little book God-speed, we commend it to the consideration of the generous and sympathetic.

S. S. R.

Dedication.

TO THE

REV. JNO. McCRON, D.D.,

Is respectfully and gratefully inscribed this Memoir.

OFTEN unto her, of whose life-history it is a transcript, has this cherished friend proven counsellor, guide, consoler—ever prompt to lend an ear, if sorrow palled the heart, and, with words of pious cheer, to point from things that are to the rich fruition of blessings in store for those who unmurmuringly drink the cup He hath given.

God fashioned the eloquent lip to speak His praise, and the tender heart to feel for the woes of humankind—ever may it be, as now, thy holy office to portray, in burning words, His omnipotence who reigneth from everlasting to everlasting, yet of whom we are told, "Like as a father pitieth his children, so the Lord pitieth them that fear him."

This feeble tribute is affection's prompting, and with it bears earnest petitions that the life which has heretofore been a bright and shining light, may continue to grow brighter and still brighter, till it be lost in the effulgence of glory, radiating from the throne of the Most High.

INCIDENTS

IN THE

LIFE OF A BLIND GIRL.

CHAPTER I.

"I WILL a round, unvarnished tale deliver."—SHAKSPEARE.

"THE web of our life is a mingled yarn, made up of good and ill together."—SHAKSPEARE.

GENTLE reader, although this will be a sad, painful story, yet it is truthful. I was born in Baltimore, Maryland, in the year 1836. My father was a tin-smith by trade, and at the age of twenty, married Sarah Henniman, a beautiful girl of eighteen summers. She was the youngest of a large family, and so loved and caressed that her youthful days passed like some fairy dream. In her girlhood she was surrounded by many admiring suitors, among whom was Dr.

G——, a very wealthy gentleman, whose offer she rejected, preferring to share the fortunes of him whom she loved with all the warmth and ardor of her heart.

After her marriage her sister sent her a faithful oolored servant, who remained with her until after my birth. My father was a man of pleasing address, and the sociality of his man ner won for him scores of friends. Every opportunity was offered him in Baltimore to have realized for himself and family a fortune, which he doubtless would have done, had it not been for his roving disposition. He was ever imagining he could double his means in some new location. He left Baltimore for New-York when I was but nine months old; two months after he sent for his family to join him. This was a trying time for my mother, to leave her relations and friends to go among strangers. Uncle Jesse, mother's youngest brother, accompanied us to the boat, carrying me in his arms. After securing us every comfort procurable, he embraced us all, and left with a fond adieu.

As we pushed from the dock, mother went on deck to gaze back upon the city where dwelt so many beloved friends, and where had been passed so many happy hours. She covered her face with her hands and wept. Little did she think she was looking for the last time upon the home of her youth. The Monumental City quickly disappeared in the distance, and she returned to the cabin to watch over her four little ones. With the details of this journey, I, of course, am not familiar, but I can recall hearing my mother say it was very fatiguing. In due time, however, we reached our destination, and were met by father at the wharf. He took us to uncle Henry W. Deems', where we remained a month.

Father then had an offer made him to go to the far West, which he promptly accepted. We were soon ready to start; it was with delight my mother left New-York, for the closeness of its atmosphere had greatly impaired the health of her children as well as herself. A long time elapsed ere we reached our journey's end, the conveniences for travel being then widely different to what they now are; railroads were the appliances of a later day.

Our first stopping-place was White Pigeon,

Michigan. The person who made father the offer failed to meet his agreement, consequently our little family were forced to depend upon his labor as journeyman, and this in a newly-settled country. We lived in White Pigeon six months, when my father obtaining employment in Shermantown, we removed thither. Here we were rather more comfortably situated than previously. Mother, being unaccustomed to hard or laborious work, felt greatly the loss of faithful Aunt Patty, our servant, whom she had been obliged to leave behind on account of her being a slave.

After living in Shermantown six months, another brother was added to our number. About this time father received some money from Baltimore, with which he purchased a tract of land about thirty miles from Shermantown, beautifully situated on the sloping bank of Silver Lake. The nearest town was six miles distant. Our land was located on the main road. About a hundred yards from the lake was a most romantic spot—a hill covered with noble forest trees, sweet birds caroling joyously their lays, flitting through the graceful foliage, every variety of wild flower bespangling the gentle ascent, with winding paths leading to the summit, where grew a gigantic oak, bowing its lofty head as though in reverence to Him who touched with beauty the cheek of the tiniest blossom blooming in Earth's garden bower. The limbs of this majestic oak bending low, took root again, and like the famed Banyan tree in India's far-off sunny clime, formed a beautiful arbor.

Our house was situated at the foot of this hill. With your permission, indulgent reader, I will outline the home of the early settler in the far West. It is built of logs, two rooms below and two above, a large open fire-place, the chimney of which is composed of sticks.

Our dwelling was rather better than that of most of the settlers. The logs were hewn and well chinked in with clay. When ready for our occupancy, mother left Shermantown with a light heart, for she felt she was going to a home of her own.

My first recollection is this removal. The Indians had set fire to the surrounding wood and prairie, and though very young, I distinctly remember covering my face with my mother's shawl to keep the smoke from my eyes. It was a frightful though a brilliant scene to behold the trees and underbrush in flames, with groups of red faces peering about in every direction. But they were friendly disposed, and insisted we should stop at their wigwams and eat some roast venison with them, to which father assented, thinking it best to keep on good terms with them. They danced with delight that the "pale face," his "squaw" and "pappooses," should sit by their fire and eat of their venison. They tried to caress and fondle me, but being very timid, I kept close to mother's side. This created much amusement among them; my fear, however, vanished ere we left them.

The next day we reached our new home, to the joy and pleasure of all. After the arrangement of our little furniture with care, we were really quite comfortable, more so than we had been since we left Baltimore. It was now November; the beauty of our home in summer was fast disappearing, giving place to autumn's deeper, richer tints. The trees had changed their verdant leafage for a reddened hue, and, though still very beautiful, touched by the early frost they seemed dreary and desolate, while the waters of the lake beating against the shore seemed mourning and wailing the departure of summer and the approach of sturdy, ice-clad winter.

My mother often sang the touching lines of "Home, sweet Home," her thoughts wandering back to the sunny South, the land of her birth, earth's most treasured spot. The very name of Baltimore was melody to her heart.

CHAPTER II.

"DARK lowers our fate,
And terrible the storm that gathers o'er us."
JOANNA BAILLIE.

"SWEET bud of the wilderness, emblem of all
That is left to this desolate heart."
CAMPBELL.

MY father's work being in the village, he was unable to come home more than three times a week, this made it rather lonely for us. After night we could see the lights from the Indian wigwams, scattered here and there through the woods. To you, perhaps, gentle reader, who have not travelled very far from home, this will seem a fearful sight; but it was not so to us; far pleasanter was it than to have looked out upon that dark forest with no vestige of living human beings near. When we had retired for the night we could distinctly hear the wolves howling, terrifying indeed was the sound—I think I shall never forget it!

But a greater and more serious trouble than this was in store for us. The times becoming harder, my father's employer discharged several of his journeymen, him among the number. At this juncture of our affairs my mother tried to contrive how she could assist in the support of our family. She could make very pretty bonnets, therefore decided to go to the village and seek employment. The next morning she made the proposed effort, and in the evening returned, having met with excellent success. About a week following, father heard he could secure work in Jonesville, nearly forty miles from home. After his departure our only dependence was upon the feeble exertions our mother was able to make. We got along pretty well for three weeks, when she was laid upon a sick bed. It was now the middle of a Michigan winter; we had no wood to burn, save the limbs of trees my two little brothers could drag from the woods, and our provisions were getting very low. A week passed, yet mother grew no better; sister Jinnie, the eldest of us five, was now in her eleventh year. It was astonishing to note the womanly character exhibited in one so young. She was our mother's nurse, as well as housekeeper. There was no kind neighbor to come in and assist us, the nearest one being two miles distant, and the snow so deep, the weather so extremely cold, it was impossible to reach those who probably would have assisted us; it was utterly out of our power to seek their aid, willingly as it might have been rendered.

At last our provisions gave out entirely, with the exception of a portion we had saved for our mother. Of this we did not inform her, notwithstanding her repeated inquiries.

"What are we to do for dinner?" said my sister one day; this was whispered in a low tone, so that it should not reach our mother's ear in the adjoining room. Brother William remembering that we had had potatoes in the cellar in the fall, replied: "Perhaps they had not all been eaten." We opened the trap-door and descended to the cellar, where, to our great joy, we found nearly a bushel of small potatoes, that had been thrown aside. We soon placed part of them over the fire to boil; when they were cooked we all sat down and ate them with salt. I have never eaten a potato since that tasted as deliciously as did those.

We now had another trouble: the provision

we had reserved for our mother was all consumed; it distressed us to think we should be compelled to inform her how destitute we were, and she so ill; a plan, however, occurred to us by which we could spare her this afflicting intelligence a few days longer; each of us had a pet chicken, which we decided should be killed for mother; sister's was the first appropriated, and in succession the others followed till all were gone.

The bushel of potatoes had quickly disappeared; alas! what were we to do! Oh! how anxiously we awaited our absent father's return. How often during that day did we go to the door to watch for him, eagerly hoping and longing to see his form in the dim distance! But alas! all that met our earnest gaze were the huge banks of snow, and the dreary waste of desolation!

That day and night passed, never to be forgotten by me.

The next morning when my sister went up stairs to perform her household duties, before she had been there many minutes, we heard a scream of delight. We all rushed up, that we might ascertain what had taken place. There stood Jinnie with something in her hands. "What is it?" "What is it?" we all exclaimed in a breath. Gentle reader, what do you suppose it was? It was nothing more nor less than a bag of garden beans, my mother had carefully dried during the summer for seed. Little did she dream they were to save the lives of her children. They were cooked, but lasted only a few days. Our pet chickens had all been killed. The pain it cost me to part with mine is indelibly impressed upon my memory; but I had only to be reminded 'twas for my dear mother, and my childish sorrow at parting with my pet vanished, giving place to real delight, that I was able to contribute aught to her necessity or her comfort.

It now became absolutely imperative our mother should be informed of the fact that all our provision had been consumed; after laying various plans by which this sad intelligence should be conveyed to her, as we sat grouped around the fire, it was finally decided Jinnie should tell her. Our dear mother was not surprised at the information, but bore it with that

Christian resignation and patience which had charcterized her throughout her sufferings.

She said if the road were sufficiently broken, Jinnie and Willie should go to the village and collect some money owing her by several ladies. Early next morning they started; on their way they called at old Mrs. Smith's, a Quaker lady, and told her of our mother's illness. She said she would go right over and see if she could do any thing to relieve her. After getting well warmed, and having another comforter wrapped about their necks by kind Mrs. Smith, they again started for the village, which they reached safely. They called on the ladies, as directed, and each paid the amount due, and one filled two baskets with provisions and groceries. It was nine o'clock in the evening ere they reached home again. Mrs. Smith was there, as she had promised. During their absence another brother had been added to our number.

Jinnie, notwithstanding her long jaunt, prepared our supper from the store she had brought with her, sent by the kind friend from the village.

CHAPTER III.

"STILL when the prayer is said,
For thee kind bosoms yearn,
For thee fond tears are shed:
Oh! *when* wilt thou return?"—HEMANS.

"DEATH found strange beauty on that infant brow,
And dashed it out."—HEMANS.

WE had scarcely seated ourselves at the table, Mrs. Smith occupying our mother's wonted place, when our attention was arrested by a familiar footstep. "Did you hear that?" exclaimed my brother Charles, looking towards the door. "'Tis some drunken Indian," responded Mrs. Smith—but we knew better, our hearts told us who it was. The door opened, and there, instead of the dark form of an Indian, stood our father, pale and emaciated. "Father, dear father!" burst from the lips of every one, and in another instant we were clasped to his bosom. Releasing us and looking about him, he exclaimed: "Oh! where is your mother?" Mrs. Smith quietly took him to her room. I will not attempt to describe the scene there enacted; the meeting was indeed one of mingled pain and pleasure.

He soon rejoined us, and we once more sat down to our evening repast, after which he explained his long absence. He had been confined to a sick bed five weeks, during which time he had sent us letters and money, neither of which we had received. We were all happy now, for father was not to leave us again that winter. He immediately ordered a plentiful supply of provision for the remainder of the cold season.

My mother's health rapidly improved, but my father had contracted fever and ague, and was quite sick for several weeks. One day, while lying upon a lounge near the fire, and rocking the cradle wherein the babe lay, mother called to him, saying it had slept long enough. He rose to see if it was still sleeping, when he found its little eyelids closed in that slumber which knows no awaking, save in the arms of Him who hath said: "Suffer little children to come unto me, for of such is the kingdom of Heaven." Our baby brother was dead! This was a terrible shock to my mother. We were sent immediately for good kind Mrs. Smith; she robed it first in life, and then in death draped its little limbs in the garments of the tomb. The next day we bore our angel treasure to the lonely graveyard, and placed him beneath the sod opposite the gently murmuring waters of the lake. The little mound was visible from our door; methinks I see it now, a mere speck amid the snow-banks; ere the morning came it was hid beneath a fleecy mantle; for my mother's sake I was glad of this, for she sat gazing upon it from her window, till the snow had quite concealed it from her view.

Her health still continuing to improve, it was not long ere we had the pleasure of once more seeing her about the house. My father, also, had quite recovered, and things bade fair to assume a brighter aspect.

It was now the first of March, and the snow was rapidly disappearing; we were very thankful for this, for the winter had indeed been a trying one to us. My father's health being entirely restored, he resolved upon returning to Jonesville to resume his work—he took me with him. His employer was a minister, one of those true souls we find here and there, in passing through the world. His family consisted of himself, wife, and two children. Little Mary North was indeed a lovely creature. We were the same age. The whole family welcomed father and myself heartily; I enjoyed my visit of three or four weeks very much, still at times was very home-sick.

My father was a beautiful singer, and of an evening numbers of persons would collect to hear him, while at his work. He would set me beside him and sing for me till nine o'clock, when he would kiss me and send me to bed. This was a delightful way in which to spend my evenings.

A few years previous to this time Mr. North had found a pot of money buried in his garden. Mary and I would search daily, that we might find one also; but our search was vain, and our golden dreams, like certain fabrics built in air, were doomed to prove visions, airy nothings only. How oft is happiness in life sought with as ill success as was sought by us the buried golden treasure; too oft is it but a cheating "ignis fatuus," deluding still and still deluding!

The day for my return home arrived; Mary had become very dear to me, we were much attached to each other, and it seemed very hard we should have to part!

We never met again; in hearing from and of her I thank God to have learned her life thus far has been a brighter and more fortunate one than mine.

It was a beautiful April day when we took the stage for homeward travel. The birds were singing gayly, the sky was bright; all earth was redolent with loveliness, the air, laden as it was with freshness, seemed fraught with joyousness. I too, with earth, and air, and sky, felt exuberant and cheerful, though I had just parted from my sweet friend Mary—for was I not seeking "home again?" place than all others most dear, and was I not soon to greet the loved ones there? Mother, sister, brothers! My very soul was filled with ecstasy!

We arrived at home; as I alighted from the stage, I was struck with the scene before me. Always greatly admiring Nature and its handiworks, I could but be impressed with the wild, uncultured beauty spreading out so lavishly; its effect upon me still recurs to memory, though years have intervened.

I have never seen Italy's far-famed sky, but I do not think it could surpass that evening sunset. The king of day sinking into the bosom of Silver Lake, the earth carpeted with the modest, fragrant violet, and the luxuriant foliage of the tall oak, swaying to the gentle passing breeze, combined to form a scene of almost fairy-like enchantment.

When meditating upon the beauties of Nature, on which I have been permitted to gaze, my heart is filled with love and reverence for the Great Being who created them. But now to me—

"All Nature is a sealed book,
Whose clasp I can not find;
It was not meant for me to read,
For I am blind, I am blind!"

I found all well and happy at home. It being spring, the Indians, according to their custom, had built their wigwams near the lake shore. They might constantly be seen in their light canoes, employed in fishing, which occupation appeared to be their chief delight. One day, while my father was absent from home, having gone to the village, I was sitting on the door-step, when looking up, I saw seven gigan tic Indians coming down the road towards our house; I was greatly alarmed, and in an instant sprang from the door into the house, and hid myself in a large oven. This was not the most comfortable hiding-place, but it was preferable to coming into contact with those wild, fierce-looking savages. I crawled near the door to watch their movements. They demanded something to eat; my mother told them she had nothing for them. On hearing this, one of them pointed to a steak which was being broiled, at the same time drawing his tomahawk from his belt and flourishing it over her head. She was very courageous, and raised the broom as if to strike him. Her bravery saved her life; instead of killing her, they turned and left the house, yelling and shouting as far as they could be heard: "White man's squaw brave!" When they had gone, I crept from my hiding-place, so completely covered with ashes and dirt, my mother could scarcely recognize me.

CHAPTER IV.

"SHE'S gone! forever gone! The king of terrors
Lays his rude hand upon her lovely limbs,
And blasts her beauties with his breath!"

DENNIS' APPIUS AND VIRGINIA.

"Good Heaven! what sorrow gloomed that parting day
That called them from their native walks away."

GOLDSMITH.

MY father who had been for some time trying to sell his land, now found a purchaser, and we were destined to be on the wing again; the necessary arrangements for a removal having been made, we bade adieu to our beautiful cabin home on the banks of Silver Lake, not without parting affectionately with our tried friend Mrs. Smith, and visiting for the last time the grave of our baby-brother.

A few days and we were located in Jonesville; for two months every thing moved on pleasantly. We had almost begun to think our troubles over, but a heavy affliction was about to befall us. Mother was taken very ill one day while all of us were at school except sister Jinnie, who sent for us in great haste—our mother was dying! We reached home in time only to receive her parting blessing. After embracing each of our little group, and bidding us be good children, loving God and one another, her pure spirit winged its flight back to Him who gave it. Our best earthly friend had left us; young as we were, we deeply felt our loss, yet the burden of our woe we realized not until years had sped away, proving how great a void is created in a child's heart and life by a mother's death! The constant yearning for her tendernesses; the quick sympathy she alone can give; the caress of her soft hand in approval; or even the mild rebuke softened and chastened, coming from her lips—these departed, life seems a very blank; then speak ye kindly ever to the motherless, ye may have power to wile their hearts from sorrow by the magic influence of a smile.

Our dear mother died among strangers, yet not unmourned for; by her pleasant and affable manners she had gained many friends who wept with us over her grave.

The time had now come for us to be separated; we were taken home and kindly cared for by friends of our mother until permanent arrangements could be made for us by our father. A lady, named Mrs. Benson, took me in charge, with whom I remained about eight months, during which time homes had been found for my brothers and sister, but as yet none for me. I shall not soon forget when my youngest brother was taken to his new home; my father went with him and allowed me to accompany them—his stranger friends seemed quite fond of him; this pleased my father very much, for he was desirous we should be comfortably and pleasantly situated. The hour came for us to part with my brother; it was very sad to leave the little fellow, but three years old, among entire strangers. The lady of the house took him into the garden, so that we could go without his knowledge. When at some distance from the house I looked back and saw Howard still playing among the flowers, I had no thought it would be the last time I should ever *see* him, though I watched him with the intensest interest as long as the faintest outline of his sweet form was visiblie.

My father's employer sent him on business to a remote part of the country; upon his return he told me he had secured a home for me with a wealthy family who had but one child, and he married. He said I should be quite a little lady, and also told me they were good religious people. I was perfectly delighted with my prospects. The day upon which I was to start arrived; the place was about twenty miles distant. Julia Benson was to accompany me. My father placed us in the stage, then got in himself, saying he would ride part of the way with us. He bade me be a good girl, to love and obey the lady who was henceforth to be as a mother to me. I held a little basket in my hand, into which he put some money, and told me to look what he had given me. While examining the contents of my basket, my father vanished; upon looking up, I discovered he had gone; shortly after I saw him standing upon the steps of the hotel we had just left; years passed, and many changes transpired, ere I met him again. In my lonely hours of musing, I sometimes recall the scene when, shortly after my dear mother's death he gathered us all around him, and talked of our approaching separation; methinks I can plainly hear the expression still: "Children, you are all together now, but may never be again" Well and fitly spoken—we never were altogether again an undivided family!

About noon of the same day we came in sight of my future home; it was one mile north of Homer, Michigan, and was a beautiful farm, well-cultured and picturesque, with commodious dwellings upon it. The stage halted at the gate, and we were met by an elderly gentleman who lifted me to the ground, at the same time saying: "Is this my little girl?" When he had led me into the house, I looked around expecting to see Mrs. Ruthven; but my new friend told me my mamma (for such he wished me to call her) was sick, but that after dinner I should see her. Dinner over, I was conducted to her chamber. On entering the room, I stood perfecty stunned with disappointment. I had anticipated meeting a kind motherly person, instead of which I saw a cold, stern woman. As she bent her pitiless gaze upon me, I thought of my own gentle mother, and burst into tears. Upon leaving the room I heard her exclaim in an angry tone: "I wonder if I am always to be bothered with other people's children!"

Time passed more pleasantly than I might have expected, in my new home. Mr. Ruthven was very kind to me, and tried in every way to render me happy and contented. I did not visit his wife's room again. After a few days I was told she was coming down to dine with us. I can not portray the awful dread with which she inspired me. The day came upon which she was to join the family at dinner, and I think I never shall forget that dinner. I could not move without her halloaing at me in sharp, angry tones. I had never been spoken unkindly to before, and this treatment almost broke my heart. Her son, George, also treated me with the greatest disdain, appearing to regard me as something unworthy his notice. He did not like his parents to speak one kind word to me, and although he called himself a Christian and a gentleman, he would stand by and laugh when his mother would knock me down. At one time from one of her blows I became senseless; when I recovered, I was lying upon the sofa, and she bathing my temples.

If they are living, and should chance to read this simple narrative, they will from it learn that the child they treated with such scorn and disdain, has scores of kind and loving friends. Oh! what a pity it is Christianity should be so disgraced, and religion be a cloak to such hypocrisy! Mr. Ruthven always treated me with the greatest consideration; he never corrected me but twice, and then it was done in such a manner that I felt a high sense of his moral obligation to me had induced him to inflict the reprimand. The cause of George Ruthven's dislike to me was on account of the property; he was afraid, were I to gain the affections of his parents I would receive a share. He tried every means to increase his mother's dislike to me.

When I had been ten months with this family I heard from my father; he had been on busness to Detroit for Mr. North. On his return, he tied his horse at the store-door, went in and settled with his employer, as was his custom, and left the house again. The horse was allowed to remain where my father had secured him, persons supposing he would return and attend to it; but after some time had elapsed, Mr. North was compelled to have the horse stabled, as my father did not again make his appearance.

It was from my friend Julia I learned my father's return to Jonesville, and of his sudden and unexplained departure therefrom. Julia, it will be remembered, accompanied me to Mrs. Ruthven's; after paying a visit of some length, she left me with my new acquaintances. Since that time she has married, and is now living in California, realizing golden dreams in that far-off pleasant land of precious ore. Cheering sunlight has shone o'er her way, while dark shadows have fallen upon mine; but 'twas His will "who doeth all things well." I will not murmur.

"Behind the clouds is the sun still shining."

CHAPTER V.

"I WILL not bow me to thoughts that breathe despair."

"OH! a cherubim
Thou wast, that didst preserve me!"
SHAKSPEARE.

"O TIGER's heart wrapt in woman's form!
How couldst thou drain the life-blood of the child?"
SHAKSPEARE.

UPON learning that my father had left Jonesville, with no communication as to where it was his intention to go, I was treated with greater unkindness even than before. The only happiness I had, was in taking care of the beautiful Evelyn, George's little daughter. I felt she was the single exception in the family who cared aught for me, as I yearned to be loved. Mr. Ruthven was kind; but his wife's dislike for me and annoyance at my presence, could but have its weight.

A lovely summer afternoon, Evelyn and I went searching for berries in a wood about a quarter of a mile from the house. We wandered on, unheeding how far from home we had gone, so occupied and engrossed were we in making garlands of flowers and admiring the gay plumage of the birds. Suddenly we were startled with the sound of distant thunder. I then observed how dark and threatening was the sky; taking Evelyn by the hand, I hurried as I thought, towards home, but unfortunately selected the wrong direction. Every thing appeared strange and unfamiliar, although I had frequently been there before. At last we reached a marsh; I fancied our home must be on the opposite side. Catching Evelyn up in my arms, I carried her across; how I ever succeeded in doing so, I can not tell, so extremely was I frightened. The thunder rolled and boomed through the vaulted heaven, the forked lightning flashed with alarming fury; it had grown quite dark, and the rain fell in torrents. Sinking well-nigh exhausted upon the wet grass, I took little Evelyn in my lap. As she nestled closely in my arms, she said: "Mamie, do you think the bears will eat us?" I shuddered at the question, they were so numerous in that vicinity; even the rain falling upon the leaves I imagined the tread of a bear.

In about an hour the rain ceased, the moon arose, and we again started in search of home; for three hours we wandered on through the thickly-shaded, dark, wet wood, ere we came in sight of a dwelling-house.

The one we at last reached was surrounded by a beautiful garden; we went to the fence, but there was no one visible; poor little Eva complained of being tired and sleepy; I laid her down on the grass and she was soon asleep—although her couch was the damp ground, and her canopy the stars of the firmament above us.

I thought I would go into the house and ask that we might remain there the rest of the night; but just as I was climbing over the fence the door opened, and a man came out; he looked like a huge Indian; I sprang from the fence, caught the sleeping child in my arms, and ran back into the woods.

Heavy impenetrable clouds had covered the moon, and we were in darkness again, the rain once more falling in torrents; we sat down under a tree, thinking we would remain there till daylight; in an instant a vivid flash of lightning darted athwart the heavens, striking and shattering a tree not far from us. This shocked us greatly, and we immediately started back to the fence; we had proceeded but a short distance, when we heard the sound of horns; we knew some one was in search of us. Imagine our delight on meeting Eva's father with a party of neighbors who had joined to aid in finding us. He clasped Evelyn to his bosom, and turning to me said: "This is all your fault." Not withstanding his unkind expression and accompanying threats, his presence had never been so agreeable to me.

It was now three o'clock in the morning, and we were six miles from home. They carried the sleeping Eva in their arms, but allowed me to walk, weary, hungry, and faint. From the effects of this exposure I was sick several days, during which time I received little or no sympathy from Mrs. Ruthven; if possible, she was more unkind to me than ever before. Oh! how I envied other children who had parents to watch over, guide, and tend them; but then "our Father in heaven" keepeth the orphan as the waters in the hollow of his hand.

In the autumn, a blind gentleman came to

board with us. He soon learned how sëvere they were to me, and often spoke decidedly in my behalf. I was frequently in the habit of leading him out for a walk, little thinking then I should some day have to be led. One day while laughing at a mistake of his, he chidingly said to me: "Take care, Mary, you may be blind yourself ere you die." How like a prophecy have the words of my old friend seemed!

Mr. Lee had lost his sight while studying law. He had a kind, noble heart; often has he taken me upon his lap, and stroking fondly and caressingly my hair, he would say in tones I well remember: "Poor child, I pity you; had I my sight you should not remain here a day longer." How I clung to him! indeed, he seemed the only friend I had in the world save the loving, gentle Evelyn.

About two miles from Mr. Ruthven's was the old Methodist meeting-house. It was here I used to attend Sabbath-school and church. During the winter protracted meetings were held, ministers and members congregating from the different parts of the country, the house always being well filled during their continuance. One beautiful Sabbath morning the entire family went to church, leaving me to keep house and prepare dinner. Mrs. Ruthven said I should cook vegetables of various kinds, and gave me numerous other directions, for she seldom allowed me idle moments even upon God's appointed day of rest. I collected and prepared as many vegetables as I deemed necessary, and obeyed her other behests as nearly as I could remember.

She returned from church accompanied by several ministers, and other persons; she looked so good, so sanctified from all sin, it seemed impossible she could ever treat me ill again. As she came into the parlor, placing her hand on my head, she said: "My daughter, have you been lonesome?" Oh! how this kindness from her made my heart palpitate. After having laid aside her bonnet and shawl, she passed out to see if I had done all she had ordered. I trembled lest something should have been left undone. In a few moments she opened the door, and called me in such sweet tones that I thought she was well pleased with the manner in which I had fulfilled my allotted task. She had scarcely closed the door upon her guests before her whole appearance changed; her sweet motherly smile gave place to a dark, foreboding frown; her voice that had been so kind and gentle became severe and sarcastic; she caught me by my hair and beat me, first on one side of my head, and then the other. To prevent my cries from being heard by the company in the parlor, she covered my mouth with her hand. After she had exhausted her anger upon me, she told me what had so incensed her: I had not prepared sufficient vegetables for dinner!

This was the usual manner in which I was treated by Mrs. Ruthven; yet the ministers who partook of her hospitality that Sabbath day regarded her as a pattern Christian. True, indeed, is the old saying: "You never know people till you live with them." Daily and hourly intercourse must either exalt or sink in our estimation those thrown athwart our way. Give to me for friends, not the loudly vaunting of good works, but the timid trusting Christian who "seeketh not her own, is not easily provoked, thinketh no evil."

CHAPTER VI.

"I LAY ill;
And the dark, hot flood, throbbing through and through me;"
"I swooned; and as I died,
Or seemed to die, a soft, sweet sadness fell
With a voluptuous weakness on my soul,
That made me feel all happy." BAILEY.

"Friend after friend departs:
Who hath not lost a friend?" MONTGOMERY.

DURING the winter I walked two miles to school, often through the deep snow. From this and other exposures, when spring arrived my health was very delicate. No one believed me ill until one day I fainted and fell to the floor. It was several days before I knew any thing passing around me. When I did regain consciousness, I learned my life had been despaired of by four physicians. Mrs. Ruthven was sitting by my bedside, weeping; it was not love for me, or sympathy, which caused her tears, it was the recollection of her cruel treatment of a lonely, friendless child. They were tears of remorse and not of sorrow. Another person was watching by me, good Elder Staples, pastor of the little frame church, where it had been my wont to go to listen to his words of pious counsel.

He asked me if I was afraid to die. I told him no; I wanted to die and go to Heaven, where I might live forever with my mother. He thought I was dying, and asked if there was any friend I would like to see. I told him no one but my father, brothers, and sister; but this was impossible, for they were far away. Elder Staples then offered up a fervent prayer for the motherless child, prayed that her soul as it winged its flight might be united with that of the pure, sainted angel-mother who had gone before to that home "where the wicked cease from troubling and the weary are at rest." He thought not then that I should outlive him. Dear departed friend! he has gone to reap the reward of his earthly labors, and to wear a crown of glory at God's right hand.

Mr. Lee at this time proposed sending for an old doctor with whom he was acquainted. His suggestion was acquiesced in, and Dr. ———

was immediately sent for; by evening he came. I felt some one touch my hand; upon opening my eyes, I saw bending over me an old man with shaggy locks and stern visage; he was shaking his head, as if in doubt as to my case. He walked to the table, and taking his medicines from his saddle-bags, prepared a dose for me. He turned and handed it to Mrs. Ruthven, at the same time saying: "Give her this: it will either kill or make her better in one hour." The mixture was given me, the doctor took the newspaper and sat down to await the result. Mr. Lee also was by my bedside, my hand held in his. By the termination of the hour the desired effect had been produced; in a few days I was able to sit up.

Different physicians had examined Mr. Lee's eyes, and their opinion was, that the optic nerve was affected; and if operated upon skillfully his sight might be restored. Accordingly he made preparation to start for New-York, and place himself under treatment of the famed oculist, Dr. ———. The day of his departure arrived. It was a great trial to me; I felt as though I were losing my only friend. They moved my chair into the porch, so that I could watch him while in sight. After bidding me an affectionate adieu, and giving me some good advice, he was assisted to the carriage. I gazed earnestly at the vehicle as it was borne swiftly over the hills. I never saw my blind friend again; shortly after his arrival in New-York intelligence was received of his death. By God's will earthly visions had been shut out from his gaze, but in yon heaven he looketh ever on beauty "it hath not entered into the heart of man to conceive."

My health was now perfectly restored. About this time Government sent the Indians to the Rocky Mountains. Near where I lived was an elevation called Black Hawk Hill, on the summit of which was an Indian trading-house, where the swarthy savages used to assemble by hundreds. The people came from the surrounding country to see them dance and hear them sing their war-songs. One day Evelyn and I, accompanied by her nurse, went to witness their performances; we had not been there long before I was attacked with a severe headache, and proposed returning home; but Eva wished to remain longer, so I said I would go alone. As I hastened down the hill, not looking upon the ground, I stumbled over a drunken Indian, lying across the path. He instantly sprang from his prostrate position, caught me by the hair, pulled me to the ground; then placing his knee upon my breast, he raised his tomahawk, and was in the very act of striking when his arm was arrested by an Indian from the thicket close at hand. After releasing me, he led the drunken fellow off to the trading-house.

It was several minutes before I recovered my strength sufficiently to walk home, so terribly was I frightened. Oh! how often have I wished when I have encountered severe trials, the Indian's weapon had done its fatal work. How much pain, sorrow, and affliction I should have been spared! But then my Heavenly Father preserved me, and his judgment is unerring.

Nothing of importance happened the following summer and winter. I went to school as I had done previously; Mrs. Ruthven and George treated me with their usual unkindness. It was now four years since my mother's death, and I determined I would leave my uncomfortable and unhappy home. I formed several plans, none of which seemed available. I thought no one would believe my simple story, for the Ruthvens had many friends, and were highly respected; but I was resolved to make my escape the following week. I knew I should have difficulty in attempting this, for I should have to complete all my arrangements, without advice or assistance, and without the family having the slightest knowledge of my intention.

I visited all my favorite haunts, to take a parting look. Near the house was a beautiful creek, where I had often strayed when weary and unhappy; its gentle murmurings and the beauty of its water seemed to soothe me. It was a branch of Great Grand River, which has always been celebrated for the blueness of its waters. The scenery about the creek was romantic and enticing. About a quarter of a mile from the house was a beautiful wood, approached by a path through the lane, bordered with wild flowers. The house was surrounded by a garden and a large orchard—indeed, a very Eden in the wilderness was the spot, yet the serpent had coiled himself amid the flowers, and his poisoning breath mingled with the fragrant odors borne from the varied tinted blossoms.

A little way down the creek on its bank was a plum tree. I called it mine; it seemed so like myself, so lonely, so desolate; there it bloomed and yielded fruitage with no other tree near. I used to think, beneath its branches should be my burial-place, that I might share its solitude. My kind friend Mr. Lee and myself, how often had we wandered to this spot, passing many pleasant hours. The tree was now covered with blossoms. Who would gather the plums when ripened? and where should I be by the time they lusciously depended from its branches?

After visiting several other dear and familiar places, I returned to the house almost sorry I had thought of leaving. But as soon as I met Mrs. Ruthven, my regret vanished and my determination became firmer than before.

The next day was the Sabbath; I went to school as usual in the morning. As I sat in my class I looked in the face of my kind teacher and was almost on the eve of opening my heart to her, and, telling her all, ask her protection. I thought of the rich and influential Ruthvens, and feared she would inform them and thus defeat my plans. No! I would keep my secret. I was now ten years old, and could do almost any kind of work. I would make my own living and be happy, which would surely be preferable to living miserably, as I now did. While indulging in these thoughts school was dismissed. After kissing my teacher good-by, I strolled through the graveyard with many a longing sigh that my head were pillowed beneath the grassy sod. I went into church, and listened to Elder Staples for the last time. It seemed the best sermon I had ever heard him preach. How true is it, "blessings brighten as they take their flight."

As I rode away at the close of the service, I gazed earnestly and fondly at each familiar object, and could scarce restrain my tears; yet—

"Why should I weep! to leave the vine,
Whose clusters o'er me bend—
The myrtle—yet oh! call it mine!
The flowers I loved to tend."

Is it strange the heart should yearn towards the inanimate in Nature, and hold sweet converse with rivulet, tree, or flower, if closed against us seem all sympathy of human kind? The heart thrown back upon itself will turn to Nature and spend its sweetness there.

> "O flowers which I bred up with tender hand!
> From the first opening bud, and gave ye names,
> Who now shall rear ye to the sun, or rank
> Your tribes, and water from the ambrosial fount?"

CHAPTER VII.

"I FLY like a bird of the air
In search of a home and a rest;
A balm for the sickness of care,
A bliss for a bosom unblest." BYRON.

"FROM this unhappy palace let us fly,
But whither shall we leave our misery?
Who to the unfortunate will kind appear,
The wretched are unwelcome every where."
CROWNE'S ANDROMACHE.

THE next morning I prepared for school, tied up a few articles of clothing, and concealed them under the fence near the road. When starting I kissed Eva. In doing so I could scarce restrain my tears. She had indeed, infused me with a fortitude from Heaven to bear up against the ills that beset my path. She was *the one star* of my *life*, and it was a great trial to part from her.

After having travelled five miles, I thought I could with safety, inquire for employment. I entered a house and asked for work. The lady looked at me, and said I was too small and delicate to do much work. She inquired my name, and I gave her my own family name, thinking there would be no danger, as I had been known ever since living with them, by the name of Ruthven. She told me she had nothing for me to do. The next place I came to, I saw a lady sitting at the window, whom I thought I had seen before, and as I did not wish to meet any one with whom I was acquainted, for fear of being conveyed back to Mrs. Ruthven's, I passed by without stopping. At a third house where I made inquiry, I met with no better success than at the first.

I travelled on till nearly dark, becoming very much frightened lest I should have to remain out alone all night. Seeing a farm-house near, I went to it and asked that I might be sheltered. Upon entering I found myself in a comfortable sitting-room, where the family had assembled for tea. This happy scene made me keenly feel my friendless condition. I tried to speak, but my voice failed, and sinking into a chair, I sobbed aloud. They all gathered round me, and Mrs. Palmer (for that was the lady's name) took both my hands in hers, and kindly asked the cause of my sorrow. It was a long time before I could speak, but when I could I told them my painful story. Upon finishing, I saw tears of sympathy in every eye, and I felt cheered when Mrs. Palmer told me, though she did not need my services, I should remain with her until I found a good home.

I had been here but a few days, when the family received intelligence of the death of a son and brother at Grand River. They were all going there, and said if I would like to go, they would take me with them; thinking it probable they would be able to procure me a home, I gladly acceded to their kind offer. I thought too, this would remove me farther from the Ruthvens, and one part of the world was as agreeable as another, so that I had a home.

I was much gratified with the scenery of the country through which I passed. At the end of two days we reached Marshall. Mr. Palmer had a friend living there, with whom he remained the night. The next morning, the gentleman's wife remarked she knew a lady living four miles distant, who wanted a little girl about my age for company, as her daughters were all away at school. Mrs. Palmer thought I had better avail myself of so favorable an opportunity offered on such pleasing terms. With regret I bade them all adieu, for they had been very kind to the lonely wanderer.

After they had gone Mrs. Simpson took me to her friend, Mrs. Stilings; this lady's appearance was very prepossessing. When Mrs. Simpson had told her my history, she came to me, and taking off my bonnet, said: "I was just the little girl she wanted to keep her company while her children were away at school."

I had only been with Mrs. Stilings a few days, when she received a letter informing her of the illness of her daughter in Vermont, and desiring her to come on immediately. More trouble was in store for me. Mrs. S. was going to send for her daughters at school to return home, and then I should no longer be desired. She told me her pastor required a little girl as nurse, and possibly I would suit, and that they were good, kind persons.

In three or four days Mrs. S. was ready to start for Vermont; her daughters arrived the night before her departure. They were both lovely girls. The day following I again started out into the cold world in search of a home. Mr. Pierson lived about a mile from Mrs. Stilings; the house was about a quarter of a mile from the main road, on a rise of ground. As I walked up the lane, very picturesque was the scene before me; the house was surrounded with locust trees in full blossom; the windows and porch were gracefully shaded with woodbine. The garden was full of sweet brier, rose-bushes, and flowers of every variety. I stood still, as though enchanted by the beauty before me, and really forgot my sad errand there. But the rough voice of the gardener soon brought to my recollection again my forlorn situation, as he exclaimed: "What do you want here, girl?" I told him I wished to see Mrs. Pierson. He said, "She was in the house," at the same time looking at me as if he wondered what I could want with her.

I pulled the bell with a trembling hand, and was soon ushered into the parlor by a servant; A lady entered; in her manner haughtiness blended with a certain show of kindness. I stated my business, also, that I had lived with her friend Mrs. Stilings. She said I should come and live with her the next week. Upon leaving I asked permission to look at the flowers, which privilege she granted. After having enjoyed this pleasure awhile, I retraced my steps to Mrs. Stilings with a lightened heart, for I had once more a home.

The next week, according to engagement, I undertook my duties at Mrs. P's. I had been there but a day or two, when she was taken very sick; just at this time the servant left. It was well I knew how to work, for with Mr. P.'s assistance, I had to do all that was to be done. Every night it would be twelve o'clock before I laid my head upon my pillow. I would then cry myself to sleep, my limbs aching, and indeed my whole body weary and full of pain. Four weeks things went on in this way, Mrs. P. unable to attend to any of her domestic duties.

One Saturday evening, after I had completed all I had to do, Mrs. P. having recovered from her illness, I asked permission to go over to Mrs. Stilings.' My request was granted; when I reached there it was dark, they were afraid to have me return by myself, and there was no one to accompany me, so they persuaded me to remain all night, telling me Mrs. Pierson would not care. It was late the next morning before we arose, and the girls begged me to go to church with them. I yielded to their entreaties, and was soon neatly dressed from their wardrobes. Service over, I thought as I had spent so much of the day away from home, I would stay till evening. When I reached Mrs. P.'s tea was over, and I could see nothing of her, for she had retired to her room. In the morning I found she had another girl assisting her to prepare breakfast. I went to slice the bread, when Mrs. P. caught me by the arm, saying in a very decided manner: "I do not wish you ever to do another thing in my house." I attempted to explain my absence to her, but she would not hear it, but told me "to leave her house." I told her I had no home, and asked her what I was to do. She said: "She did not care—it was not her look-out."

I went to my room, and throwing myself into a chair by the open window, gave myself up to harrowing, painful thoughts—What shall I do?

Where shall I go? Who next will give me a home? O father! why do you leave thus alone and friendless your child? Why not come to me?

While thus musing, Mrs. P. sent for me to come to breakfast, but I could eat nothing in her house after she had spoken so unkindly to me. I tied up my little bundle of clothing and was soon ready for another start. I went to Mrs. P., and asked her to pay me for what I had done; she gave me two dollars, saying: "That was more than I had earned." I left the house, not knowing where to go; sitting down on a log by the roadside, and gazing up and down its length as far as eye could reach, my heart grew sick, for I knew that in either direction there was no one to care for me.

CHAPTER VIII.

"GENEROUS and righteous is thy grief, slighted child of sensibility;
For kindness enkindleth love, but the water of indifference quencheth it;
Thy soul is athirst for sympathy, and hungereth to find affection." MARTIN TUPPER.

"OH! dark, dark, dark, amid the blaze of noon,
Irrevocably dark, total eclipse,
Without all hope of day!" MILTON.

"KNOW, he that
Foretells his own calamity, and makes
Events before they come, twice over doth
Endure the pains of evil destiny." DAVENANT.

IT was a lovely June morning, the birds were merrily caroling their lays in the tree above my head; scattered here and there at my feet was the beautiful wild pink, and not far off a rose bush laden with its fragrant blossoms which at another time I should have gathered and placed in water; now I plucked and threw them from me, so mocking seemed they in their beauty. Yet the voice of the sweet birds raising high their tuneful notes, cheered me, and I arose from my seat by the roadside to continue my wanderings, but my brain reeled and my limbs refused to support me. When again conscious, I found myself upon a bed surrounded by curtains; drawing them aside and looking out, every thing appeared new and strange; there was no person in the room. I made an effort to rise and walk to the window, but I was too weak; just at this moment a lady entered. I asked her where I was; a pleased expression passed over her countenance upon finding me able to make inquiries concerning myself. She informed me I had been quite ill for more than a week, but that I had found friends, and they had taken good care of me.

I asked how I came there, but Mrs. Downly refused to tell me until I was stronger. In two weeks I was quite well again, when I learned the particulars of my illness. Mr. Downly, while passing in his carriage, saw me lying on the ground; he thought me dead, but upon examining my pulse, found I had fainted. He lifted me into his carriage, and conveyed me to his wife.

A physician being called in, he pronounced my disease congestion of the brain, caused by some great shock to my nervous system.

My new friends, as may be supposed, were anxious to learn my name and history, which, when recovered, I narrated to them, not omitting Mrs. P.'s treatment; at this they were greatly surprised, for knowing her well, they had not thought her capable of so much harshness. They had believed her a Christian, one who revered and kept the holy injunctions laid down upon the sacred pages of the book of books. Mrs. Downly said I should remain with her until I was eighteen, at which time I would be better able to take care of and provide for myself.

The rest of the summer passed very pleasantly. Mr. and Mrs. D. were kind, and I felt a guiding Providence had instructed my steps towards their door. But a greater trial than any I had as yet endured was in store for me. It was now the last day of August. I was sitting at the front-window admiring the beautiful sky, so clear, so apparently transparent, one might have fancied they could have gazed through it into the far-beyond. So pleasant was it I turned from the window and thought to enjoy a walk in the garden. Upon opening the door, I was greatly astonished to see rising rapidly in the distance, one of the blackest clouds I had ever beheld. While watching its approach and heavy gathering masses, I called Mrs. Downly to come and look at it; she said there would be a violent thunderstorm, and we hastened to close the windows and doors securely.

I still stood watching the heavens, changed as they were; there was no sound of thunder, no flash of lightning. Little thought I that dark portentous cloud would be the last my vision would rest upon. Like a thing of power, it stalked through the sky and then disappeared. Contrary to our expectations no rain followed. I am not superstitious, but I have sometimes thought that mighty moving shadow was a premonition of the terrible cloud about to settle down upon the horizon of my life—burying all things in thick darkness.

Towards evening of that long to be remembered day, I was attacked with severe pain in my eyes, yet I could not discover that they looked differently from what they usually had.

The light of the candle caused me great pain, and before retiring I observed the lids were very much swollen. I suffered intensely with them that night, and by the morning they were pain fully inflamed. I had constantly to be wiping them to be able to see at all. They continued in this way until noon. I went to the looking-glass, and after wiping them about five minutes I could see distinctly. They then closed, and in less than twenty-four hours I was blind! forever blind!

The doctor was sent for; he prescribed a lotion, the application of which caused acute pain, and seemed to afford little or no relief—indeed, it did more harm than good.

Every neighbor far and near advised a remedy, a number of which were tried during the following two weeks, my eyes still continuing to grow worse. Finally, a lady who in riding out was caught in a storm, and came into our house for protection, offered to effect a cure if I would return home with her. M s. D. informed her of my friendless situation. Mrs. Weller said she would take me with her and make every effort to have my sight restored; and that I should remain with her as long as I desired. We started; a seven miles' drive brought us to Marshall. It was here Mrs. Palmer had sent me out alone and unprotected six months previous. How great a misfortune had befallen me in that time! Mrs. W. treated me with every kindness, and employed all the means in her power to effect the restoration of my sight, but in vain; the inflammation instead of abating continued to increase.

When I had been with Mrs. W. a month, the whole family was taken sick with the ague and fever; so ill were they, one could not wait upon the other, and worse than all, we had no means of support, for we depended upon Mr. W.'s labor, and he was prostrated with the chills. Their parents lived about twenty miles in the country, and they were compelled to go home to them to be taken care of. Mrs. W. said she would take me with them, and we all set out for Clarence. It was now the last of October.

We had not travelled many miles before Mr. and Mrs. Weller were attacked with chills; the jolting of the carriage and the heat of the sun had given me a violent nervous headache. Mr. W. was so ill he could scarcely drive. It was quite dark when we reached his mother's door, The old lady came out and helped one after another from the carriage. Upon seeing me she asked: "Who is this you have with you?" Mrs. W. told her I was a little blind girl who had been living with them, to which information her mother replied: "Well, I think you had enough of your own to bring home sick without other people's." At the same time she was as kind to me as to her own children, and lifted me as tenderly from the carriage. I did not wonder at her expression after I had entered the house; her daughter and husband and child were lying sick, having arrived the day before.

As soon as we had taken off our bonnets, the old lady made me lie down while she bathed my head and temples with cold water, and placed a soothing poultice on my eyes. I can not portray the agony of dependence I experienced that night; my friends were kind, very kind, but I had no claim upon them. Their acts of tenderness and consideration caused my tears to flow and my heart to ache with a keen sense of desolation. But though

> "The reed in storms may bow and quiver,
> 'Twill rise again;"

while the oak of a century may be riven by a single blast.

We were one mile from Mrs. Weller's father's, and on the morrow we went there to remain for a while. Arrived at this second destination, we found Mrs. Clarke, Mrs. W.'s mother, quite ill. Mr. C. was a Quaker; he took me by the hand and said, "I am sorry for thee, my dear," but his wife said: "She did not know what they brought me with them for." I did not mind her saying this, she was quite an invalid, and I thought when she was better she would feel less annoyed at my being there. Mr. C. was extremely kind, and tried in every way to prevent my feeling uncomfortable or dependent. He said he thought he could cure my eyes, and after he had consulted the physician of the place, he would do what he could. The next day the doctor came; he directed me to be kept in a dark room for four weeks, with bread and molasses as diet; besides this, I had every second day to undergo an operation upon my eyes giving me the most intense and excruciating pain.

Just at this time another physician hearing of my blindness, called to examine my eyes; upon inspection he gave it as his opinion they could be cured, and my sight restored in three weeks. I was willing to endure any amount of suffering to be able once again to see. They were so sensitive, I could not bear to touch them with the softest handkerchief.

The doctor prepared a compound of dissolved alum and rum, and raising the eyelid applied to the eyeball a linen cloth saturated in the wash; this was so painful, I fainted while submitting to it. After I recovered I would not let him touch the other eye, which made him very angry, and he cursed me bitterly. Upon leaving the house I heard him say: "*I hope she will never see!*" He has had his wish! I have never seen aught above or around me since that time.

"With the year
Seasons return, but not to me returns
Day, or the sweet approach of even or morn,
Or sight of vernal bloom, or summer's rose,
Or flocks, or herds, or human face divine;
But cloud instead, and ever-during dark
Surrounds me." MILTON.

CHAPTER IX.

"I STRIVE to sing and smile, but ah! there presses
A gloomy pall upon me—I am blind." AMELIA WELBY.

"A BEAM of comfort, like the moon through clouds,
Gilds the black horror, and directs my way." DRYDEN.

"BE strong to hope, O Heart!
Though day is bright,
The stars can only shine
In the dark night." PROCTOR.

"AND whispers are heard full of Nature and Truth,
Saying: 'Don't you remember?'" ELIZA COOK.

As I have before stated, Mr. Clarke had said he could work a cure for me; the efforts of the two doctors having failed, he thought he would at least try and allay the inflammation.

He went to the woods and dug some roots; of them he made tea, which I was to drink, also to apply externally as a wash. In two weeks I was greatly relieved, the inflammation had disappeared, yet I could not see. So great blessing was denied me, and it became my duty to bow to His will who, had it been best for me, could have decreed: "Receive thy sight." Life would indeed, have known less of trial, had my vision been restored, but His ways, though inscrutable, are wise, and I fain would with an unmurmuring heart submit to that which he has seen fit should befall me—praying:

> "—— Wisdom at one entrance, quite shut out,
> So much the rather, thou Celestial Light,
> Shine inward, and the mind through all her powers
> Irradiate, there plant eyes, all must from thence,
> Purge and disperse."

Mr. Weller finding there were no hopes of my regaining my sight, grew very weary of me. He and Mrs. Clarke were constantly telling me how dependent I was, sometimes treating me with the greatest unkindness, and threatening to send me to the poor-house. This terrified me greatly, as I had always imagined it a dark, dismal prison. In this part of the country there were officers appointed to look after the sick and the friendless, and if a certain amount would cover their necessities and the services of a physician, these were rendered; if not, they were sent to the almshouse. To one of these officers

Mr. Weller applied in my behalf. A few days after, while lying upon the sofa, two gentlemen came in and inquired for me. The truth flashed upon my mind. I begged and entreated them not to take me to the poor-house. Mr. Cook, one of the gentlemen, lifted me from the sofa and held me caressingly and tenderly in his arms, quieting my fears by telling me "he was not going to take me there, but that he had brought a doctor to examine my eyes." This was done, but the result was futile—he could but decide they were incurable.

I clung to Mr. Cook, afraid he would leave me. I told him how unwelcome, and what a burden I was considered by those with whom he found me. He asked if I would like to go home with him. I could only answer with a flood of tears, not of grief, but of overflowing joy and thankfulness. He lifted me into the carriage, and we drove to his home. It was now the 15th day of January, and I was in my twelfth year. I had been blind three months. Late in the afternoon we arrived at our journey's end. Mr. C. conveyed me from the carriage to the door, where we were met by his wife. She took me kindly by the hand, while Mr. C. told her who I was, saying: "Fannie, I have brought this poor child home to live with us; we have seven children, but I think we have bread enough for them and her too; take her, dear Fannie, and be as a mother to her." I could feel that she was weeping tears of sympathy for me. Taking me by the hand, she led me into the warm parlor and seated me in a cushioned rocking-chair by the fire. She said I was "too thinly clad for that season of the year, and it was a wonder I had not frozen, so scantily supplied."

She told me she had five daughters and two sons, and just then they came bounding in, a band of joyous children. They were surprised to see me, but their mother informed them who the little stranger was, and that she was going to live with and be one of their family, and they must love me as a sister. They kissed me affectionately, and divided with me their toys. Benjamin, the oldest of the group, tried in every way to amuse and entertain me. Such kindness was more than I could bear, and tears would come in defiance of all effort to restrain them.

The next morning I found a suit of new and warm clothing prepared for me. After I had dressed, and Mrs. C. had carefully curled my hair, I was much improved in appearance; so great change had a single day with my new friends made in me.

To employ my time, it was proposed I should learn to knit; at first I thought this impossible as I could not see, but they persuaded me to try. Often when I would become impatient at my slow improvement, and almost in vexation, would toss my knitting from me, Mrs. C. would pick it up, repair my errors, and cheerfully say to me: "Mary,

"'If at first you don't succeed,
Try, try again.'"

Her sweet and encouraging tones would inspire me with a still more earnest desire to accomplish my task. In about a year I learned to knit a pair of stockings, and I assure you it was no small gratification to me, my acquired knowledge.

The children were all fond of reading; nothing gave them greater pleasure than to read aloud to me. Whenever Benjamin found a book he thought I would like, he would await some opportunity when I could listen while he afforded me so agreeable a pastime.

I became so accustomed to the house and grounds, I could walk about without a guide, even go to a neighbor's quite alone. I was never happier than when I had done any little thing to please my benefactress; she would always most generously reward my every effort. It was part of her faith to commend a child when it had done well, thereby inducing a future endeavor to deserve a kind word or approving smile.

Mr. C. had a brother living in the village who had a blind daughter, named Almeada, a year younger than myself. We became much attached to each other, and spent a great deal of our time together.. I had also another friend in the village, Elder Hobert, a Methodist minister; with him and his family I passed many happy days. On one occasion he presented me with a copy of the Bible, which I still have, and from which I often have read to me a verse he marked: "Him that cometh unto me, I will in no wise cast out." He has since gone to California, but is still my friend.

Being now able to knit pretty well, I felt anxious to do something towards supporting myself. I thought I would ask one of our neighbors to let me do the usual winter knitting her household required. These arrangements I had planned in my own mind; when I communicated them to Mrs. C., she rather dissuaded me from making the attempt, fearing it would be more than I would be able to accomplish. In the afternoon, however, the lady of whom I had thought, came to our house, and I asked her to let me do her knitting. She appeared pleased with my desire to do something towards making a livelihood, and said I should come to her house and knit by the week.

The next morning I entered upon my engagement. My remuneration was a dollar a week. From this time I could command as much and more than I could possibly do, and in this way supported myself for four years.

I was very sorry to be away from Mr. and Mrs. Cook, and the children, they had been so kind to me. The first week I missed them all sadly. Only an orchard lay between Mrs. Wilson s and their farm; every morning I would take my seat in the front-door just as the sun was rising, and listen for the dear familiar sounds from Mrs. Cook's yard; but the sweetest far, were the tones of her own loved voice. I longed to be with them all, yet more earnest was my desire not to be a burden to my friends. I felt an honest pride in providing for myself while I had health and strength.

I had been with Mrs. Cook three years, when I received a letter from my sister in Chicago, stating she was married, and for some time had been trying to gain intelligence as to my whereabouts. She had found brother Charles, and he was living with her, and she wished me to join them. It seemed so singular I should receive a letter from my sister, not having heard from any of my family for so long a time. I was very desirous to see her, but felt as though I could not tear myself away from my dear friends who had so faithfully supplied the place of father, mother, brothers and sisters. We corresponded for two years, she urging me in every letter to come to her. Finally she sent me a paper containing the advertisement of a celebrated oculist, said to be performing almost miraculous cures in Chicago.

This decided me to attempt the journey. I had been with Mr. and Mrs C. five years, and had had no opportunity of procuring skillful treatment of my eyes. Hope once more bid me anticipate a morrow, when should be removed the misty veil and I again *see*. I resolved to go to my sister and place myself under the advice of this famed oculist.

CHAPTER X.

"I TRAVEL all the irksome night,
By ways to me unknown."

MONTGOMERY.

"FROM the sad years of life,
We sometimes do short hours, yea minutes, strike,
Keen, blissful, bright, never to be forgotten,
Which through the dreary gloom of time o'erpast,
Shine like fair sunny spots on a wild waste."

JOANNA BAILLIE.

"AND whether we shall meet again, I know not;
Therefore, an everlasting farewell take:
If we do meet again, why, we shall smile;
If not, why, then this parting was well made."

SHAKSPEARE.

BY the second week in January, (a fortnight after my determination to go,) I was ready to start. The day of my departure Mrs. Cook took me into her room, where we were joined by Mr. C. Both gave me much good advice and counsel; their every word was carefully treasured in my memory, and has often been retrospected since that time.

They told me I had been a good girl, and had never done any thing to displease them; they also said, if they had ever spoken unkindly to me I must forget it. They thought it natural I should desire to be with my sister, but assured me if I needed a home their door would be open to me and a hearty welcome ready. If I at any time required assistance, I was to write and let them know, and it should be forthcoming.

The sleigh now made itself heard by the merry jingling of the bells; but they sounded not joyously as was their wont. They seemed the parting knell of the fond associations I had cherished. The final moment came; how can I describe what to me was so fraught with anguish? Mr. Cook accompanied me to the cars; before we were one mile from home the weather was so extremely cold, my cheeks were frost-bitten, and I had to hold snow to them to draw the frost out. We soon reached the depot, and Mr. C. procured me a comfortable seat by the stove. He then bade me good-by and left me. Once again I was a lonely wanderer among strangers. How devious has been the way by which I have been led!

We travelled but slowly on account of the snow-banks that covered the track. No one spoke to me during the day except the conductor. Just as evening was setting in, the cars ran into a snow-bank eight feet high; they tried to force their way through it, but this attempt was about half-completed when they could get no farther. We were within a quarter of a mile of Kalamazoo. The conductor informed us it would be impossible for the ladies to get out, and that the gentlemen would have to crawl out and procure fuel and provision for us. He said they had sent to Marshall for another engine to extricate us from our difficulty, but it would not be there before morning. I was not alarmed, as I had learned there was no real danger. My seat by the stove was very comfortable, and my carpet-bag contained plenty of refreshment, thanks to my thoughtful friend, Mrs. C. While I was sitting thinking of the dear ones I had left, the pleasant home where they were, even then, doubtless, speaking kindly and tenderly of me, a gentleman came to me, and opened a conversation by inquiring how I liked the probability of being snow-bound till morning; also asking me if "I were near-sighted." I told him "so much so I could not see at all." He then offered to take me under his protection until we were removed from the snow-bank. I thanked him, and told him how glad I was to meet with a friend. He took a seat by me, and entertained me by narrating similar misfortunes during his travels. He thought we were very fortunate to be so near a town.

My friend told me he was on his way home to see his mother, whom he had not seen for seven years, and I in turn, informed him I was going to visit a sister and brother I had not seen since I was a very little child. We became quite sociable; it seemed as if I had always known him. Our attention was now drawn to a comical Yankee among the passengers, who was amusing them by relating various adventures he had had. His appearance was as grotesque as his conversation was ludicrous: his pants were of almost every color, his vest of variegated calico, and, besides a buckskin coat, a pair of nondescript boots, he wore an old slouched hat distorted into the most inconceivable kind of shape. After having entertained us for some time, he arose from his seat and exclaimed: "The rules say you must not put your feet on the cushions, but they say nothing about keeping a fellow all night in a snow-bank." Having made this speech, he so arranged two of the seats as to make a pretty comfortable couch, and throwing himself upon it was soon in the land of dreams, snoring most sonorously, no doubt in unison with the fancies flitting through his brain.

The passengers were becoming weary of conversation; my kind friend urged me to feel no delicacy in reclining my head upon his shoulder. I thanked him, but refused, partly because he was a stranger, and then I did not feel very drowsy.

At two o'clock the locomotive arrived, running against us with great force, almost pushing us through the bank. The shock was so sudden, it quite discomposed our Yankee friend, throwing him from his sleeping-place, and part of his temporary accommodations with him. He sprang to his feet and, looking much frightened, exclaimed: "Golly, have they got snow-banks in this ere world, too?" The passengers burst out laughing. He told us he had dreamed he had been killed and had awakened in another world.

I was now becoming very weary, and Mr. Chamberlain proposed making me a bed upon a sofa in the ladies' saloon, to which I readily assented. Several gentlemen offered me their buffalo-robes; with these and one of the cushions, I soon had a very comfortable napping-place. When I had lain down, Mr. C. threw a buffalo-robe, he had nicely warmed by the stove, over me, and then left, bidding me rap and he would come to me, when I had refreshed myself with as long a nap as I might desire.

I was soon fast asleep, and do not know how long I might have continued so, if I had not, in making an effort to turn myself upon my very narrow couch, rolled from it on to the floor, making a terrible noise. I was almost as much frightened as was my chance friend, the Yankee. Mr. Chamberlain soon had the door unlocked, to ascertain what had happened. He laughed heartily on hearing I had fallen from my bed. He led me again to my warm seat by the stove.

It was now nine o'clock; the morning clear, cold, and frosty; and there were no prospects of our being extricated from the snow-bank that day. The water in the engines had frozen, and had to be thawed before any probability could exist of effecting a removal. The gentlemen went out and procured for us provision to last the day. Had I been his sister, Mr. Chamberlain could not have taken better and more tender care of me. When I would thank him, he would say: "I am doing no more than I would wish any one to do for my sister, were she situated as you are." He asked me if I was fond of reading. I told him I was. He then brought several books and passed the remainder of the day reading to me.

At nightfall we were not much nearer starting than the evening previous. It was very wearisome waiting so long; the delay seemed very tedious. What little sleep I had, was upon Mr. C.'s shoulder; my slight timidity in availing myself of his kind offer the night before, having entirely vanished: his kindness and gentlemanly attention had won my perfect confidence. He told me, "Several of the passengers had asked if I was not his sister," and that "he had told them I was, and said I should tell them the same if any inquired of me." The next morning, while Mr. C. was absent from the car, ordering our breakfast, a lady took a seat beside me, and after preferring a great many questions, she asked: "If the gentleman with me was my brother?" I answered as I had been instructed, upon which she remarked: "I knew he was, for he looks exactly like you." So much for family resemblances.

That afternoon we left the cars, Mr. C. and myself, and enjoyed a comfortable dinner at the hotel, thinking it preferable to remaining longer where so many shared accommodations. We also spent the afternoon at the hotel, as the cars were not to start till evening. While sitting upon the sofa, my friend came and sat by me, and taking my hand in his, said: "Miss Mary, I have been travelling the last seven years, and have met with a great many ladies, but have never seen one who interested me as you have." I told him: "I did not know what I should have done had I not met with him."

We passed the afternoon in pleasant conversation: he relating his travels and consequent adventures, some grave and some gay. We were startled by the car-whistle, and hurried to regain our former agreeable seat by the stove. The weather had greatly moderated since morning, and there being quite a vigorous fire in the stove, I felt myself fainting. I remembered Mr. C. trying to open the window, and then became perfectly oblivious to all around me, until upon recovering, I found myself out upon the platform supported by the arm of my friend, while with the other hand he was bathing my temples. Several ladies were standing by, anxious to render some service. The first words I heard were: "Sister, do you feel better now?" To which kind inquiry I responded with my heart rather than with my lip, for his tenderness really seemed the gentle ministering of some good Samaritan.

The passengers were all delighted to be once again on the move, and a glad huzza went up as their farewell to Kalamazoo. Nothing further of importance happened until we reached Niles, at which place a man got into the cars and took a seat just back of us. He disputed loudly with the conductor about paying his fare; from this and other indications, we soon discovered he was intoxicated. After he had paid his fare, and the conductor had passed on, he slapped me on the shoulder in a very rude manner, at the same time saying: "My pretty miss, you had better take a seat round here by me." Mr. C. sprang to his feet in an instant, exclaiming: "Villain, what do you mean by insulting my lady? if you do not take a seat in some other part of the car, I will pitch you out into the snow-bank." To my great relief he acted upon Mr. C.'s threat immediately.

At one o'clock, we reached Michigan City, where we were to remain till morning. When the cars stopped, Mr. C. told me to sit still while he went out and attended to our baggage. He had been absent but a few minutes when a man stepped up to me and asked if I was not going to a hotel. I informed him I was, as soon as my friend returned. He said I had better go with him. I declined. He insisted upon my doing so, and asked if the gentleman with me was my brother. Just then my noble friend came up, and I felt greatly relieved when I found him near. While walking to the hotel, he inquired what the man whom he saw speaking to me had said. I repeated to him what had passed between us, and he informed that though I did not know him, it was the same man who had been so insulting tc me in the cars, and that if I had gone with him, he would never have seen me again. I felt his arm tremble as though with indignation.

We had reached the hotel, where we procured supper. On going to the parlor the next morning, I found Mr. C. alone. He arose and seated me; then said we would have to part, for he was compelled to take the stage, for his home twelve miles distant. He frankly told me he would not leave me until he had placed me in charge of my friends, but that his money was expended, leaving him barely sufficient for the remainder of his journey. He offered to place me under the protection of some one who would take equally as good care of me as he had endeavored to do.

CHAPTER XI.

"HEAVEN gives us friends to bless the present scene;
Resumes them, to prepare us for the next."

YOUNG.

"JOY! the lost one is restored!
Sunshine comes to hearth and board."

HEMANS.

"ABSENCE, with all its pains,
Is by this charming moment wiped away."

THOMSON'S AGAMEMNON.

MR. CHAMBERLAIN left me to institute a search for some one travelling in the same direction I was. He soon returned with a gentleman, whom he introduced as Mr. Hicks. He was very polite, but did not make so favorable an impression upon me as had my first friend. The bell rang, the signal "All aboard" was given. Mr. C. having procured me an agreeable seat, and wrapped me in Mr. Hicks' buffalo-robe, left me with the parting injunction not to forget him, and to write as soon as I reached my journey's end. He had checked my baggage and bought my ticket, indeed had paid all my expenses since I met him. I offered to pay him, but he refused, saying I must find some other appropriation for my money. Again he told me I must never forget him, which injunction was all unneeded. I could not cease to recollect and cherish kindness such as he had tendered. He had pressed my hand for the last time and was gone. I wept as if indeed I had parted with a beloved brother.

Mr. Hicks was a Californian, and shortly after we had started, seven other Californians joined him and took seats by us. On observing I was blind, they each gave me a gold dollar, which Mr. H. said I would do perfectly right to accept. The Central Railroad at this time did not go through to Chicago, and we had twenty-five miles to travel by stage. Offering the amount for my fare, I was told it had already been paid by the gentleman who had previously been so generous to me. It was now mid-day, and we were seated in the stage to complete our journey after the fashion of "auld lang syne." We got along very well; I had dined while waiting for the stage, therefore did not feel as wearied as I otherwise should have done.

It was nearly dark when we reached the City Hotel in Chicago. Upon alighting from the stage a gentleman stepped forward and offered to pay my fare; I thanked him, but told him it had already been attended to. Mr. H. secured a room for me, while he went out in search of my friends, who had not been informed as to what time I should be with them. While he was absent, I made my toilet with more than usual care, as my brother and sister had not seen me for so many years—indeed, since I was a child.

Not far from the hotel Mr. H. met a young man, of whom he asked if he could direct him where to find a person by the name of Charles Day. Singular as the coïncidence may seem, that was his name. Mr. H. informed him: "His sister had been placed under his protection part of the journey to Chicago, and that she was at the hotel." Without waiting to hear another word, he hastened to meet me, and we were once more clasped in a loving, fond embrace. "Is it possible this is my darling sister?" were his first words. He kissed me over and over again. After remaining with me a short time, he left, saying he would soon return. I wondered at his not taking me with him instead of desiring me to remain alone until he should bring our sister.

Reaching sister's he said: "Jinnie, who do you think is at the City Hotel?" "I do not know," was her reply. "Why, sister Mary!" "How does she look?" was her first inquiry. "Look! I wish you could see her," said Charles, "she's an awful-looking somebody; she has hair as red as fire, with hand and foot as large as mine, I do believe, and then too, she is awkward and ignorant." "Was she well dressed?" said sister. "Well, I think she had a faded calico on." But my dear sister resolved as far as pos sible to remedy all deficiencies, though she could not change the color of my hair, or the size of my hand and foot, as represented by my mischief-loving brother. Charles was commissioned to go for and bring me home, as sister could not well leave her family.

After he had started on his errand, Jinnie's husband was informed of my arrival; and it was thought best to prepare their servant for my very unprepossessing appearance.

A short ride, and I was at my sister's home. I knew nothing of what had passed as to my personal or mental endowments, nor cared I. It was happiness indeed, once more to be near those so dear to me; and clasped once again in a loving sister's embrace. After Charles had led me to the parlor, he ran away to his own home, not far distant, for he had been some three weeks married. Sister neglected to introduce me to her husband, in her haste to take my bonnet off to ascertain if my hair was really red; after having duly examined it with a light near by, she presented him to me; he greeted me most cordially and affectionately, saying: "He was glad to have a sister, for he had never had one."

When somewhat rested and refreshed, he entered into conversation with me, to ascertain how ignorant I was, I suppose. I narrated to him the incidents of my journey, not omitting the many kindnesses I had received. While so doing I afterwards learned Ellen, the Irish girl, peeped in through the open door at me. When sister went out to give directions for tea, she exclaimed: "Why, what a story-teller Mr. Charles is; why, she's a real lady, and she hasn't got red hair, nor large feet and hands neither!"

Sister and I sat up nearly the whole night, recounting our past lives, and all the hardships we had endured since our dear mother's death. She had undergone almost as numerous vicissitudes as I had. At the age of sixteen, however, she was married to one of the best of husbands; thus finding a protector and counsellor who had tenderly shielded and guarded her.

The next morning Charles came in and offered me one of his gloves to try on. The joke was then told me, and I with the rest laughed at the very comical representation he had given of me. My wardrobe was examined by sister, and pronounced somewhat out of date.

In a few days Doctor ——— was called in to examine my eyes; he pronounced them incurable; this announcement made me very unhappy, for I had hoped to find relief. Shortly after this, Dr. ——— was consulted. He professed to have performed great cures, and thought he could in my case do the same, but that it would require three months' treatment, occasionally operating—also placing me under a regular course of medicine.

I was quite hopeful at the prospect of regaining my sight; and once again being able to look out upon this beautiful world, filled with the handiwork of the Most High. According to appointment Dr. —— with several students, came to perform the operation; he desired the presence of the latter, that they might benefit watching so delicate an effort of skill. It was extremely painful, almost more than I could bear, but hope buoyed me up. And as a sort of balm or soothing palliative, just as it was over came a letter from Mr. Chamberlain, in answer to one I had sent, informing him of my safe arrival, also of the contemplated operation upon my eyes. A week only elapsed between the forwarding of my letter and the receipt of his answer. Three months passed, and my vision was neither restored nor improved.

The close atmosphere of the city, and the expenditure of physical strength the operations upon my eyes had occasioned, had told fearfully upon my health; indeed, it seemed utterly shattered. Oh! how I longed to be once more in my country home. Sometimes I would think I would go to Mrs Cook, and never leave her again; but then this would not be treating with proper consideration the kindness of my relatives. Every second week came a sweet and welcome letter from Mrs. Cook, affòrding me unutterable delight.

That long tedious summer passed, leaving me delicate and frail. Sister Jinnie, Charles and Mr. Barton, were all attentive to me, and if affection and tenderness could have reïnstated my health, I should not long have been an invalid.

CHAPTER XII.

"The joys of meeting pay the pangs of absence."
Rowe's Tamerlane.

"And doth not a meeting like this make amends
For all the long years I've been wandering away?"
Anon.

"I can not speak, tears so obstruct my words,
And choke me with unutterable joy."
Otway.

"Oh! art thou found?
But yet to find thee thus!"
Vespers of Palermo.

"Ah me! what hand can touch the string so fine!
Who up the lofty diapason roll
Such sweet, such sad, such solemn airs divine?"
Thomson.

My brother-in-law was a carriage-maker, and carried on the business in Chicago, Charles being his partner. One day, while Mr. B. had left the shop to go to dinner, a very gentlemanly young man entered and inquired of Charles if Mr. N. A. Barton were in. On being told he had gone to dinner, he took a seat as if to wait his return.

Charles asked him: "If he wished to get some work done; if he did, he was Mr. Barton's partner, and could arrange matters with him." The gentleman then said: "He had not called to have work done, but he had heard Mr. Barton was his brother-in-law, and had come to ascertain if it were true." Charles looked at him intently for a moment, and then exclaimed: "Is it possible this is William Day? If so, we are brothers, for I am Charles Day." The truth needed no second confirmation; in an instant they were in each other's arms and no words can justly represent the joy of that meeting. Mr. Barton entered the shop, and Charles with pleasure beaming in his countenance, introduced his long-lost brother William. He welcomed him heartily, for he was anxious our family should be reunited.

Sister and I were sitting in the nursery; Mr. B. came in and told us a gentleman in the parlor wished to see us. We went down immediately; on entering, Mr. B. asked sister if she had ever seen his friend before. To which she answered that "she thought not." The stranger then said: "Have you forgotten your brother William?"

We both ran to him, and were most fondly held to his heart. He seated me upon his knee, and gazing into my face discovered I was blind! Oh! the anguish of that moment. Large tears of sympathy rolled down his manly cheeks, and in speechless agony he pressed me to his bosom.

When his emotion had sufficiently subsided to allow him to speak, he bent over me and in low soft tones whispered: "Sister, it is the will of God, it is all right." This calmed my wildly throbbing heart, and I felt I could submit to my affliction, although forever shut out from me was the face of him I so dearly loved, save as memory had portrayed it years ago. I could say: "Thy will and not mine be done, O Lord!"

Four of our long-separated family were now reünited. Where were the remaining two? Father and brother Howard? Where had they wandered? Unchecked the wish arose that they ere long might be added to our group.

Until a late hour that night we were recapitulating the various scenes of our lives. We found each had suffered, but mine had been the most heavily clouded, and was too sorrowful to shadow our first evening together. Nor will my father, brothers or sister know all it fell to my lot to endure, till they scan the simple story contained in these pages.

Brother William told us he had been living in Racine, Wisconsin, the last nine years, with the same persons with whom father had left him. He had always been treated by them with great kindness; indeed they had been like parents to him. In a few days he departed from us to return home, promising to make every inquiry concerning Howard, our youngest brother.

Upon bidding me farewell he placed in my hand twenty-five dollars, telling me to give it to my doctor, it might encourage him to do his utmost to restore my sight.

Fall and winter passed; my sight was in no way improved, and my health was declining. My sister was now keeping a large boarding-house, and I must not forget to mention the many kindnesses of the boarders to me. There was one in particular, whose attention and friendly offices I shall ever remember. He made constant sacrifices of his leisure to sit by me and read or write for me. He also frequently entertained me by playing on the flute, in which he was quite skilled: his favorite melody too was the one my dear departed mother so much loved, "Home, sweet, sweet Home." Often have I been soothed listening to the plaintive strains, for they recalled her angel presence, yet ever as the dulcet notes would die away would come the sad truth, she had left me, never to return. Oh!

"I miss thee, my mother! thy image is still
The deepest impressed on my heart,
And the tablet so faithful, in death must be chill,
Ere a line of that image depart."

One bright day during that spring, while brother Charles was walking down Randolph street, he met a youth who inquired of him where Mr. Barton, a carriage manufacturer, could be found. He told him he was then on his way there, and if he would accompany him he would conduct him to the gentleman's establishment.

As they walked along, the stranger informed Charles he had just arrived in the Michigan cars, and was entirely unacquainted in the city. On reaching the shop, and brother indicating to him which was Mr. Barton, he stepped up to him and said: "Do not think me impertinent if I ask the name of the lady you married." Mr. B. told him. Virginia Day. To which the stranger replied: "She is my sister." There was a second affectionate greeting in that shop between brothers, after which they came to the house. Sister was in the parlor; on hearing the door open, she looked around. Her eye rested a moment on the stranger, when with an eager cry of joy she sprang towards him, exclaiming: "O Howard! Howard! my darling brother!" She brushed the hair back from his forehead, and gazed with pride upon his noble countenance.

At this time I was confined to my bed, and sister in speaking of me narrated to him my great affliction. With extreme caution they informed me of his arrival. He came to my room, and when clasped in those manly arms I could scarce believe it was the little brother I had parted from years before.

In a few days I was able to sit up; we sent for brother William. He came, and the hour we had so longed for had at last arrived. We were once again a united family save the presence of our father. All thought him dead except myself. I always felt we should meet again. Brother William after spending a few days with us returned home, brother Howard remaining to learn a trade with Mr. Barton.

Like myself, he had met with much unkind treatment. The persons with whom father placed him after a short time elapsed, cast him off, not caring what became of him. He was anxious to acquire knowledge. As soon as he was large enough to work, he toiled early and late to earn sufficient to purchase clothing, pay his board, and during the winter season attend school. In this way he received a fair education, and is now in Iowa, engaged in business for himself.

My health continuing to decline, my brother in Racine sent for me to pay a visit, thinking a change might be beneficial to me. The second of September I started. Mr. Barton took me to the boat, and seated me in the cabin. A gentleman came up to me and asked if I had consumption. I told him I hoped not. Taking a seat beside me, he examined my pulse and informed me I would not live three months if I continued the treatment I had been undergoing. He then invited me to walk on deck. The day was beautiful, and Lake Michigan calm, peaceful, serene. I had not long enjoyed the open air and sky before I felt refreshed; my spirits also became quite enlivened, Dr. Clark was so agreeable and entertaining. He was on his way to Milwaukee, but said he should stop long enough at Racine to see me safely with my friends. Brother William met me at the boat. The doctor did not bid me good-by till I was seated in the carriage. Then he bade me adieu, hoping I would soon regain my health. I never exchanged words of friendship with him again, but in my heart his memory hath a sunny nook.

CHAPTER XIII.

"Thy voice is sweet as if it took
Its music from thy face." Miss Landon.

"And should'st thou ask my judgment of that which hath most profit in the world,
For answer, take thou this: The prudent penning of a letter." Tupper.

"Lay her i' the earth;
And from her fair and unspotted flesh
May violets spring." Shakspeare.

Brother William took me to Mr. St. Clair's, the family by whom he had been reared. They welcomed me as cordially as if I had been their own child. The next day brother told me he was engaged to be married to one of the most beautiful ladies in Racine, and that he should bring her to see me. He did so, and I thought he was correct in thinking her very lovely. Her low, sweet voice fell like music on my ear, and from that moment I loved her.

I could fill whole pages, reciting the hospitality and kindness of the people of Racine to me, during my stay among them. I remained four weeks. My health being much improved, I again returned to my sister. The journey back was rather unpleasant; the weather was stormy, the lake rough, and I confined to my berth, terribly sea-sick. About nine o'clock at night, I reached home.

On the following day Dr. Norfolk came to see me. I told him I did not desire his services any longer, as I thought my sight would never be restored. He grew very angry, and left the house, saying he should send his bill. In the afternoon it came, and was one hundred dollars. I sent him word by the servant I would never pay it, for I had already given an equivalent for his services. In a few days I was summoned to court. I was very much frightened, having never been sued before. Mr. Barton bid me not be alarmed, he would see the matter properly adjusted. The day arrived on which the trial was to take place. I was so nervous and frightened I could not walk to the court-house. I can not describe my feelings while seated in the large court-room surrounded by so many people. When, however, I thought of the cruel manner in which Dr. N. had treated me, my strength returned, and I gave in my testimony without faltering.

The Dr.'s witnesses were sworn. Just as the last one took his seat Dr. ——— entered. He walked up to me and examined my eyes. He was then sworn, and testified, it was the worst piece of mal-practice he had ever met with. His opinion had great weight, for he was considered one of the best physicians in the city. The case after a few days' litigation was decided in my favor.

My brother was not satisfied no further attempt should be made to effect the restoration of my sight, therefore Dr. Shipley was consulted, the best Homeopathic physician in the place. He made no promises, held out no false hopes, but said he would do the best he could for me. At the end of the year under his treatment I found my health and sight much improved, being able to distinguish light and colors.

My sister was the only one of our family who remembered our relatives in Baltimore.

She had written to them, but the letters had remained unanswered. The Doctors all advised me to go to the New-York Infirmary, so I concluded I would write to my relatives and, informing them of my misfortunes, ask their assistance. I mentioned my intention to brother and sister, but they opposed it, so I determined to arrange my plans without their knowledge if possible. Sister had a servant who could write; the next Sunday I took her to my room, and dictated a long letter to my uncle Jacob Day, my father's only brother. I secreted it until an opportunity transpired of sending it to the post-office. My friend of flute recollection mailed it for me, promising not to mention the circumstance to any one.

It had been nearly three years since I had left Mrs. Cook's, and I was now making preparations to go and spend a few weeks with her. My little niece was to accompany me as far as her grand-parents in Marshall. Mr. Barton placed us in the cars, and his father was to meet us. The journey would have been a pleasant one, but I was taken quite sick soon after starting.

When we reached Kalamazoo, I thought of my friend Mr. Chamberlain, and listened eagerly, hoping to hear his voice among the passengers. At twelve o'clock we arrived at Marshall. To my great relief we found Mr. Barton awaiting us. I was by this time so ill, it was with difficulty I reached Mr. B.'s. After taking some refreshment I felt better.

Little Cora was delighted, having never been away from home before. When the sun had gone down, taking Cora by the hand, we proceeded to call on my friend, Almeada Cook. I felt scarcely able to get there, although it was only four squares distant. No one knew me except Almeada; she recognized my voice as soon as I spoke, and appeared delighted that I had come back again, and begged me to promise never to go back to Chicago.

It was now getting dark, the evening was beautiful, calm, and peaceful, with no sound of dissonance—indeed, only the birds were heard as they fled homeward each to its leafy bower. As I walked along, meditating upon the many changes that I had transpired in a few years, I forgot Cora was unacquainted with the streets, and soon found she had turned a wrong corner, and I was unable further to direct her. She became dreadfully frightened, fearing we should never find the way home. Meeting a gentleman, we inquired of him. He kindly offered me his arm, which I gladly accepted, for I felt scarcely able to walk; and through his graceful and prompt attention we safely reached Mr. Barton's.

The next morning Mr. B. accompanied me to Mrs. Cook's. When at the gate I asked him to let me go in alone. I found the sitting-room door open and Mrs. Cook and her five daughters engaged sewing. I walked in without knocking and not one of them knew me. I then said, O Mrs. Cook! have you forgot me? and in another moment my head was pillowed upon her bosom, and I was nearly smothered with kisses from the girls. I visited the little room which had once been mine, and found every thing just as I had left it, indeed nothing appeared changed, except the girls had grown to be young ladies. Old Lucy still reigned supreme in the kitchen, and talked and laughed, and gave wise counsel as sagely as ever. My favorite seat under the old oak still remained. I forgot I was sick while exploring my former home and its treasured haunts. Mr. Cook and Benjamin, on coming in to dinner, welcomed me most cordially as the others had done before. Mr. C. said he was sorry I had ever left them.

The next morning I was so ill I could not rise, and continued growing worse. The doctor having been sent for, after seeing me pronounced my symptoms those of typhoid fever. He told Mrs. C. I was dangerously ill, and he thought could not live. He said my constitution was so broken down, and the disease so firmly rooted, it could not possibly be removed. She begged him to do his utmost to bring about my recovery. For my part, I was happy in thinking I would die in my old loved home, and be buried in the quiet grave yard on the hillside.

After a few days they wrote to sister, telling her if she wished again to see me in life she must come immediately. As she sat weeping over the letter, my friend, the strains of whose sweet melodies reach me even now, inquired the cause of her distress. She handed him the letter, after glancing over it he exclaimed: "Go to your sister this very hour; I will take you to the depot and do any thing else you may desire." He then went out to call a carriage; after ordering it, he stopped at his office and wrote me a letter, just such a one as only a true-hearted friend could write.

That afternoon they laid me upon a sofa in the parlor. I had not been there long when sister Jinnie and little Cora entered. Cora ran and threw her arms around me and said: "O Aunt Mary! don't die, don't die." This excitement was too great for my weakened nerves, and I fainted. Sister had a carriage prepared with a bed in it, to take me to Mrs. Barton's. After the sun had set, they lifted me to the carriage and placed me in it; Mrs. Cook arranging my pillow with all a mother's tender care. How like a mother had she seemed to me in my desolate orphanage, and yet twined even with the memory of her tendernesses will come the sweet lines of the poetess:

"I miss thee, my mother, when young health has fled,
And I sink in the languor of pain;
Where, where is the arm that once pillowed my head,
And the ear that once heard me complain?

> "Other hands may support me, gentle accents may fall,
> For the fond and the true are still mine:
> I've a blessing for each; I am grateful to all,
> But whose care *can* be soothing as thine?"

My loved friend Mrs. C. having made me as comfortable as she possibly could, embraced me for the last time; for shortly after, ere we met again her pure spirit went home, she bade adieu to earth that in heaven she might reap the reward promised unto the faithful. Her mission here had been fulfilled, and she is even now one of that shining throng who surround the Throne, and who are ever singing in rapturous strains: "Unto Him who has washed us and made us white in the blood of the Lamb, be honor and glory forever."

CHAPTER. XIV.

"Sow; and look onward, upward,
Where the starry light appears—
Where, in spite of the coward's doubting,
Or your own heart's trembling fears,
You shall reap in joy the harvest
You have sown to-day in tears." PROCTOR.

"We must part awhile; and our love will be
The fonder after parting—it will grow
Intenser in our absence, and again
Burn with a tender glow when I return."
PERCIVAL.

The ride, though a short one, exhausted me very much, and it was many days before I recovered from the extreme weakness and prostration consequent upon it. Contrary to my expectations, however, as well as to my physician's and friends', I did again rally, indeed sufficient to undertake the journey back with sister. All were delighted to see me, for they had not thought to do so again. Two or three days after our return, sister came into my room, bringing with her a missive from Baltimore. Uncle Jacob Day had received my letter, which he had handed to my cousin William Henry, and the letter sister had brought me was from him. He said he had shown my letter to all my friends, and they deeply sympathized with me; that he would have sent me money immediately, but not knowing me he was afraid of imposture; but if I could borrow the amount necessary to defray my expenses to Baltimore, he would repay it with interest and I should never want for friends. He also said, if any thing could be done to restore my sight, expense should not be spared.

I was so delighted on receipt of this letter, that I was quite an invalid for two days. In about a fortnight I was ready to start for Baltimore, my mother's native place. A day or two before leaving Chicago, sister gave me a party, inviting all my intimate friends and associates, many of whom I shall never meet again; a number of them died that fall with the cholera. My chief regret in parting with my sister and brothers, was the delicate health of brother Howard; when I parted from him I feared it was forever, but God has seen fit to spare him to us and restore his health.

Monday was the day fixed for my departure; on Sunday we were all together, and the time sped rapidly away. The next evening at nine o'clock I went to the cars, accompanied by my brothers and sister. They were very unwilling to have me travel such a distance alone; but so anxious was I to go, I would not wait for company. As the cars were not to start for half an hour, sister said she would take the seat opposite me, and when she saw some person whose appearance pleased her, she would offer it to them; for she rather prided herself upon her powers of discrimination, in this particular.

She had not long remained on the look-out, before observing a lady and gentleman enter the car, she arose and transferred the seat to them; Mr. Barton inquired how far they purposed travelling. The gentleman said as far as Toledo. He then asked if they would take me in charge while our route continued the same? This they promised to do. After procuring me a through-ticket and placing me in charge of the conductor, when my new friends should have left me, my brothers and dear sister bade me adieu; most affectionately telling me they should expect me to return to them again in a few months.

When alone and the cars were moving off, I began to realize the extent of my undertaking and the loneliness of my situation. As we whizzed past the city limits, I felt I was leaving every one I knew on earth to seek the protection and friendship of strangers. Would they be kind to me? I would repeatedly question myself. I tried to banish these feelings, and place implicit trust in Providence.

My companions did not converse much, and of this I was glad, for I preferred communing with my own thoughts. We travelled on in this way till twelve o'clock, when I was aroused from my reverie by a sudden crash, which I learned was occasioned by a train from an opposite direction having come in collision with us. It threw our train off the track, and entirely demolished both engines, but fortunately no one was injured. The conductor came in and told us he had sent back to Milwaukee for an engine, and we would not be able to start before m rning. After the accident one of the passengers went about the car stamping his foot, and declaring the collision had wakened him up all except one foot. This created a laugh among the passengers.

It was seven in the morning before we were on our way again. At twelve that day we reached Toledo. When the cars stopped, the gentleman and lady of whom Mr. B. had asked some attention to me, arose to leave. I handed my carpet-sack to the gentleman, when he refused it, saying: "The conductor will come and see to you after awhile." They then left, and in a few minutes every passenger had gone. One of the workmen put his head into the window and said: "Young lady, you had better leave the car, for the train is going to start back in a very little while." I asked him if he would not come to me, I wished to speak to him. I then told him I would like to be conducted to the parlor of the hotel. Placing my sack on his arm, he took me by the hand, and literally dragged me over the seats until I began to think my life was in danger. He meant kindly, I'm satisfied; he was good-hearted, only rather rough.

He led me in this way to the parlor, where were other of the passengers, to whom he said: "Ladies and gentlemen, I want you to take good care of this young lady, for she is in the dark sure." While saying this, he held a tight and firm hold of my arm, seeming to apprehend some intention on my part to run away from him.

I had just removed my bonnet and shawl, when the bell rang for dinner. No one offered to assist me, and touching a gentleman, (if such I may term him,) on the arm, I asked him to assist me to the table. He walked away without taking any notice of my request. I spoke to five or six others, all of whom treated me in a similar manner. I then sat down, thinking I would go without my dinner; but I found this would be impossible, for I was very weak for want of refreshment, having eaten nothing since the night before. All had left the parlor except one lady. I asked her if she would lead me to the dining-room; she replied very coolly and indifferently: "I am not going out to dinner." I told her I would pay her for her trouble if she would take me out. She said she wanted no pay, and then walked with me to the dining-hall, and left me in care of one of the waiters, who, by the way, paid me every attention. 'Tis not always the finest broadcloth covers the most noble or manly heart. A lady who sat next me at table was very kind; after dinner she took me to the ladies' dressing-room, where I arranged my toilet, and we then went again to the parlor. The conductor came to me, saying I must excuse him having neglected me, he thought I was in care of the lady and gentleman sitting near me, and did not require his services. He offered to send a gentleman to wait upon me across the river to the cars. At three o'clock this gentleman came, and the instant I heard his voice I felt I had a friend. He kindly inquired if my journey had been pleasant? I told him how neglected and lonely I had felt. He said he was not surprised at this, for a rougher or more uncivil set of persons he had seldom seen. I could not forbear repeating to him the opinion of my travelling companions which I had formed from overhearing their conversation. I really thought them extremely domestic and rural in their predilections, as they had talked of nothing but their pigs and potatoes all the way.

We had now reached the cars; my friend informed me he was agent on the railroad, and would be able to remain with me the distance of sixty-five miles. I was much pleased with this intelligence; for though sister had been prepossessed with the appearance of the gentleman and lady, under whose charge she left me at Chicago, I felt sure Mr. Dennison would prove far more agreeable and attentive. He was during the short time we travelled together all I expected he would be from my first impressions, and I was really very sorry when, arriving at his destination, he bade me adieu.

He advised me to remain in Cleveland a day or two, as I would be exhausted from my jaunt thus far. He introduced me to a friend of his, whom he said would render me any service I required; he also gave me his card to hand to a Mr. Chase, when I reached Cleveland. I invited Mr. D. to call and see me if ever he came to Baltimore, which he said he should certainly do. I felt grateful to him for his kindness, and did not wish him to think I should soon forget it.

Upon arriving at Cleveland, which we did at

nine o'clock in the evening, I acted upon Mr. D.'s advice; and desiring a carriage, the friend with whom he had left me called one, and we drove to the Chase House. The proprietor met me at the door with a cordial "How do you do?" Indeed, so cordial was this inquiry, I almost fancied he must be some old but half-forgotten acquaintance. Leading me into the parlor, he asked where I was journeying. I told him to Baltimore, to have my eyes examined and to undergo treatment, hoping to recover my sight. He said I need not go any further than his house for that purpose. I asked him if he was a doctor; he told me no; but that his son had performed some wonderful cures. He then gave me a room, and in half an hour returned and waited upon me to supper. Supper over, I was introduced to his son, of whom he had spoken. I was equally well pleased with him as I had been with the father.

He proposed examining my eyes in the morning, to which I assented. They then kindly invited me to spend the remainder of the evening in their private parlor with their family. Upon examination the day following, the doctor pro nounced my eyes as being curable, stating that in a few weeks, if I would delay my trip to Baltimore that long, he thought a restoration of my sight could be effected; but this was impossible, situated as I then was.

The doctor inquired if I was fond of music. On my telling him I was passionately so, he seated himself at the piano and performed most delightfully. All the family treated me most kindly, and I shall ever cherish for them sentiments of lively gratitude for their many attentions to me during my brief stay with them.

CHAPTER XV.

"I MAY be kind,
And meet with kindness, yet be lonely still." LANDON.

"I KNOW not how it is;
But a foreboding presses on my heart,
At times, until I sicken." PROCTOR.

"WHY didst thou fling thyself across my path?
My tiger spring must crush thee in its way,
But can not pause to pity thee."

SOMEWHAT rested and refreshed from my respite from travel, I started at three in the afternoon to complete my journey. As Mr. Chase helped me into the carriage he said: "It really made his heart ache to have me go alone." But I assured him I could get along very well, for I was not easily discouraged. Dr. Chase accompanied me to the cars; upon leaving me he also expressed concern lest I should meet with some unpleasantness. I assured him I was not apprehensive but some one would send me on from any other stopping-place I might have; no one would desire to detain me very long. He bade me good-by, saying he should expect to see me back soon.

At six o'clock we reached Lyons, where we changed cars. The conductor took me to the hotel, telling me not to leave with **any** one else, as he would return for me—we were to start in half an hour. The time expired, and I heard one train after another, move off—all the passengers had quitted the parlor except one gentleman. I inquired of him if the Pittsburgh train had gone; he said they had started fifteen minutes before, and he thought there would be no other until morning. Shortly after, he took the cars for Cleveland, and I was left entirely alone. Just as I was thinking what I should do next, a gentleman came in. He asked me if I had been forgotten; I told him I was in care of the conductor, and that he had left me, bidding me wait till he returned for me; that I had placed perfect confidence in what he had said, and through having done so, the Pittsburgh train had started without my knowledge. He said the conductor had told him of the circumstance, and was very much troubled about it, but that another train would arrive in about three hours, and he would remain with me until it came. I thanked him, but plainly signified I preferred being alone. Upon this intimation he went out and was gone two hours; they seemed the longest I had ever known. The intense heat of the atmosphere and the innumerable musquetoes were almost beyond endurance. When the gentleman returned, I laughingly, though in a decided manner, informed him he and the conductor were one and the same person, (his voice had discovered him to me the moment he had spoken,) also remarking that doubtless he was surprised I should know him again: "Oh! do you forgive me?" he exclaimed. "I never had any thing so to worry me in my life. There were some Germans who detained me so long paying their fare, the cars moved off, and I only had time to jump from them, which I did in order to repair my apparent neglect of you."

The remaining hour he entertained me by reading the daily news. At last the train came, and I was introduced to and placed in charge of Mr. Higgins—again at the mercy of a busy, bustling conductor. He appeared a kind and fatherly old gentleman. When conductor number one was about to leave me, he asked if I expected ever to come that way again. I told him, if I should, certainly not in care of any of his forgetful fraternity.

Mr. Higgins arranged me quite a comfortable couch, appropriating his coat and my carpet-sack, then spreading a large shawl over me, said I could sleep all the way to Pittsburgh. Every time he would pass by, he would hold the lantern close to my face and say, "Poor child, poor child," thinking me asleep.

At one o'clock we reached Pittsburgh. I regretted parting with Mr. H.; he kindly offered to place me in care of the conductor of the next train. The following morning I was scarcely able to rise; an old lady who had roomed with me, observing my weakness assisted me to dress, and was as tender and solicitous as if she had been my own mother.

After paying my fare I found I had exhausted my means, for I had not prepared a sum adequate to the expense occasioned by the various delays I had been subjected to. I resolved not to allow this to trouble me; I had a through-ticket to Baltimore, and would make directly for that point, hoping to reach my friends the next day. But in this I was doomed to sad disappointment; my troubles were not yet over. The old lady travelled with me seventy miles, when, bidding me good by, she hoped the rest of my journey would be free from accident, or any untoward circumstance.

Soon after her departure, a person took the vacant seat behind me, so perfumed with musk, his close proximity nearly took my breath. Being very thirsty, I turned and asked the fragrant, highly-scented gentleman if he would be so obliging as to procure me a glass of water? To which request he made answer: "There's the water, can't you help yourself?" On my informing him I was blind, he said: "He was not in the habit of encumbering himself unnecessarily when he travelled." A gentleman sitting near, overhearing the colloquy, brought me a glass of water. When I thanked him he said: "He had done no more than any gentleman ought to do for a lady."

The conductor coming into the car, brought

the unwelcome intelligence that we would be compelled to remain in Harrisburgh all night, as there was no train leaving for Baltimore before morning. Oh! I can not describe my feelings on receiving this information! I had no money and knew no one living in Harrisburgh. What to do or how to act, I did not know. My head began to ache violently, and I felt as if my strength were leaving me. I would have relinquished all the hopes to realize which I had travelled so far, endured so much, to have been once again by my sister's side, at home. At this moment the train stopped and about twenty happy school-girls entered the car in which I was sitting, feeling so lonely and desolate. Their gayety and mirth but increased my sense of misery. I could not decide how it would be best to act on reaching Harrisburgh. A single beam of hope bid me fancy I should meet some one as generous and kind as Mr. Chase had been, but in this I was disappointed.

It was nine o'clock when we arrived at our destination for the night. The conductor passing, I spoke to him of my embarrasing situation and told him, if he would procure me accommodations at a hotel and defray the expense, the amount should be refunded by my friends, immediately after my arrival in Baltimore. He told me to sit still till he had got through with his business, and he would then attend to me.

I remained in my seat as he had directed, till every passenger had left the car, and the lights had all been put out; still no conductor came. At that moment I felt friendless, helpless, and penniless. I was aroused from this painful reflection by the impertinent voice of the conductor saying: "Well, sis, what must I do for you?" I shuddered to think I was in the power of this man, for it seemed to me I could hear the villainy in his voice. He asked a great many questions, all of which I answered in monosyllables. I repeated my request that he would take me to a hotel, to which he replied: "There were some very kind ladies living about a mile distant, whom he knew, and who would be very happy to have me stay with them over night, or indeed a whole week if I liked." I told him I should prefer stopping near by, as I wished to be in good time for the morning train. He said: "There was no hotel near." This I knew to be false, for I had heard the gong sound for supper, and it seemed to be directly opposite. He then said, after I had informed him of my impression, "Oh! yes, that is the ——— ——— Hotel," and that he would walk over with me, and ascertain if the landlord would accommodate me for the night. Upon my taking his arm, he asked: "What made me tremble so?" I told him, "I was very tired," for I did not wish him to know I was afraid of him. When we had reached the hotel he took me in, and then sent for the landlord; he told him I had a through-ticket to Baltimore, but owing to several delays, my money had all been expended. "Oh! I understand," said the landlord. "She is welcome to the best my house affords." Then the conductor took him out into the hall, and they held a whispered conference, continuing about five minutes, and I could not avoid feeling a foreboding that it was concerning myself, for the conductor's actions appeared to me very singular and suspicious.

The landlord returned to me, accompanied by the chambermaid, saying he would wait on me to my room. The girl led the way, and I followed with him; he left me at the door, telling me he would call at my room in half an hour, that I might go down to take some refreshment. After the girl left me I locked my door, and commenced a thorough investigation of every nook and corner. I should not have been at all surprised in my search to have put my hand on the conductor. The evening was extremely warm, yet I lowered my only window, fearful lest some one might be able to make their way in through it.

I had just completed my toilet when I heard a rap at my door. In answer to my inquiry: "Who was there?" I recognized the voice of the landlord. On going out, I asked him to wait till I locked my door. As I put the huge key in my pocket he laughed as if he wondered what I had to lock up so securely.

He treated me with the greatest kindness during supper. After having enjoyed this repast I was soon again safely locked in my room. When I arose the next morning, I felt much refreshed. After I had arranged my hair and dressed, hearing some one in the hall, I thought

I would ask them to take me to the parlor. I attempted to unlock my door but could not succeed, it would not yield to my efforts. I thought I was locked in, and that at the conductor's instigation. I searched the wall of my room for a bell-cord; on finding one I gave it such a terrible pull, it brought the girl in quite a hurry. I told her I could not open my door; she pushed violently against it, and it flew open. I had unlocked it and it had required some such force only as she had rendered to "open sesame." So in one instance, at least, I had done the conductor injustice—he had not locked me nor had me locked in my room. The chambermaid took me down to breakfast; just as I had finished, the landlord came to me, and said the train for Baltimore would leave in a few minutes. I hurried on my wrappings and went with him to the cars.

After seating me he left, saying I would have no more changes to make, and that he had put me in care of the conductor. He had no sooner gone than I felt a presentiment of something wrong, and asked a lady near me if we were on the Baltimore train. She said, No! we were on the Newport train. I caught up my carpet-sack and ran out on the platform without assistance. Taking hold of some man's arm standing there, I said hurriedly: "I want to go to Baltimore!" He lifted me off the cars though they had commenced moving, and put me down on the platform. There I stood alone—no one to appeal to, to learn whither I should go. But a gentleman passing by, observing my helplessness, offered to place me in the train I desired; and I felt greatly relieved that I had escaped that wicked conductor, for I always believed he was to have gone to Newport with the train that morning. His whole demeanor was to me inexplicable.

CHAPTER XVI.

"In all my wanderings through this world of care,
In all my griefs—and God has given my share,
I still had hoped, my long vexations past,
Here to return—and die at home at last."

GOLDSMITH.

"Oh! still my fervent prayer will be,
Heaven's choicest blessings rest on thee."

MISS GOULD.

Two o'clock in the afternoon we reached Baltimore. I can not describe the emotions with which I entered the city; its very name, from associations with a loved mother's memory, was dear to me. It had been her girlhood's home, and now she lay buried far away. I had returned to the place of my birth, which I had quitted years ago, an infant in my mother's arms. I could not forbear a hurried survey of the past, and with the teeming recollections of the moment there came a more vivid consciousness that—

"There is none
In all this cold and hollow world, no fount
Of deep, strong, deathless love, like that within
A mother's heart!"

Yet with these memories of the past were blended surmises as to my future. I was in Baltimore a stranger, though in search of friends. The conductor having ordered me a carriage, I directed the driver to take me to the Fountain Hotel. When there, the landlord treated me with great kindness. After dining, I lay down to rest myself before sending for my cousin, from whom I had received the letter encouraging my coming to Baltimore.

Requesting an interview with the proprietor, my nap over, I told him whom I wished to see, and asked him if he could inform me as to his residence or place of business; he consulted a directory, and ascertained the latter. I then sent him information of my arrival. It was nearly dark when a servant came to my door and told me a gentleman wished to see me in the parlor. Knowing it was my cousin, I desired the servant to direct him to my room. During the short interval ere he came to me, I walked the floor in nervous excitement, and a hundred thoughts chased each other in lightning succession through my mind. A rap at my door—I tried to open it, but my strength had fled; I felt utterly powerless. All I could do was feebly to say, "Come in."

The door opened, and my cousin was with me. He took my hand in his, and in a kind, friendly voice said: "Is this Miss Mary Day?" Upon my assenting, he remarked: "Then I suppose we are cousins." He led me to the window, for it was getting dark. I asked him if "He thought I was an impostor;" he said, "No! you look too much like my mother for me to think that; she has not a child who resembles her as strongly as you do."

He then inquired concerning my journey, and said he had not expected me before receiving another letter. He left me to go down and settle my bill at the hotel, and returned in a little while to take me home with him. We were not long reaching his house; after taking me into the parlor he said he would go and communicate my arrival to his family.

While alone, I sat musing on how strange and vision-like it seemed that I should be in Baltimore, and had met for the first time my cousin, and how different I had found him, to what my conjectures had been. I also wondered what sort of person his wife would prove; would she welcome me cordially as he had done? perhaps she was proud, and would not sympathize with me in my affliction. These reflections made me very unhappy, and at that moment how gladly would I have returned the weary distance that lay between my absent brothers and sister and myself.

In the midst of my gloomy fancyings, Cousin William again came to me, this time accompanied by three lovely children, to whom he introduced me as their cousin Mary. This cheered me, and made me feel less desolate. He then informed me his wife was in the last stage of consumption, which was the reason she had not been down to meet me.

This sad intelligence he had scarce communicated when the door opened, and I heard a soft step approaching. Cousin William arose and introduced his wife as my cousin Sarah. As she kissed me affectionately, I felt the burning fever on her cheek. I shall never forget the soft sweet tones of her voice, as she said: "I am glad you arrived safely, Cousin Mary." Very musical sounded this welcome to me, for it seemed the echo of a loving spirit. Oh! how bitterly I had felt I had wronged her in allowing the wayward fancies in which I had indulged concerning her. She indeed, it seemed to me, must walk the earth with a peculiar grace, an angel at the home-hearth unawares.

The evening glided most delightfully by; Cousin William quite surprised me with the long list of relatives whom he informed me were anxious to see me. When I retired for the night, Cousin Sarah kissed me "good night," at the same time saying "she hoped my troubles were all over."

The second evening after my arrival, while sitting at the tea-table, Cousin William read me the advertisement of a physician who professed to have wrought great and marvelous cures. The paper stated he could be found at his office, corner of Fayette and Exeter streets. While talking the matter over, an aunt and another cousin came in—Aunt L., my mother's eldest sister. She held me tenderly to her bosom and wept over me. As soon as she could speak she said: "Is it possible this is Sarah's child? I must take her home with me this evening."

To which I acceded, after obtaining Cousin William's consent, also his promise to consult the oculist whose advertisement he had read; for I naturally felt intensely anxious to benefit by his skill, if in my case it were likely to prove efficacious.

As we passed along Asquith street, Aunt laid my hand upon the house in which my parents lived last in Baltimore. The spot seemed dear to me, for though years had fled, it had once been familiar to one who now lay in the cold churchyard. The walls had once echoed her footsteps, and her voice had there been heard.

Uncle L.'s family consisted of six persons, and I was received cordially and affectionately by them all. Cousin Maria, Aunt's daughter, I learned, was a widow; her two children, Frank and Mattie, were very interesting girls; they all resided with Aunt, which made it very pleasant for me to be with them. They seemed desirous to anticipate my every wish, and did every thing in their power to amuse or interest me.

The next day Cousin William called to accompany me to the doctor's; Mattie went with us. After he had examined my eyes he said he could restore my sight in six weeks. Cousin

William was delighted at the probability of my being able to see again, and said he would give any amount if he wrought a cure. The doctor bathed my head with some kind of liquid until I became so weak I could not speak a word nor help myself. He then blew another liquid into my eyes, which occasioned me great suffering for an hour or more. Cousin William all the while stood by, whispering soothing and encouring words in my ear.

I was under treatment six months, daily undergoing the most acute pain. Cousin William paid eight dollars a month to the doctor, besides defraying my boarding expenses at Aunt L.'s.

My health had greatly improved; indeed seemed perfectly restored, for which I felt most thankful. My friends appeared never to weary rendering me kind offices. Former acquaintances of my mother lavished upon me the friendship and attention they had in years gone by bestowed upon her.

One day Cousin Maria while walking out with me proposed we should try and find Aunt Patty, our old and faithful servant. She was living with her daughter in Potter street. When we went in, Cousin asked her if she had ever seen me before, or any one who looked like me. She led me to the window, the better to decide as to her answer, for she was getting old and her sight was growing dim. She thought she had, but could not recall where. Cousin then told her who I was, and that I was blind. She caught me in her arms, the dear, good, kind old creature, and wept over me like a child. As soon as she could speak she said: "If ever any one went to heaven, it was Miss Sarah, surely." She then showed me various presents my mother had made her, and which she seemed to prize as relics sacred and invaluable. Among them was a Bible which she promised should be mine at her death, but said she could not part with it before, for she had through it learned there was a heaven to obtain, and studying its pages had found Christ had died to save her. She had learned to read it for my mother's sake, and it had been the instrument of her soul's salvation. After passing two hours listening to Aunt Patty's praises of my mother, which were as incense to my loving heart, we again turned our steps towards home, having promised often to visit her in her snug little domicile.

CHAPTER XVII.

"OH! not in cruelty, not in wrath,
The Reaper came that day,
'Twas an angel visited the green earth,
And took the flowers away." LONGFELLOW.

"THUS sometimes hath the brightest day a cloud."
SHAKSPEARE.

"OH! grief hath changed me since you saw me last,
And careful hours, with Time's deformed hand,
Have written strange defeatures in my face."
SHAKSPEARE.

MY cousin Sarah's health was now rapidly declining, and her sweet babe was fading like a flower by her side. She was only confined to her bed three weeks till the Destroyer came. I visited her every day. She would converse with me when her strength permitted, and her thoughts and words already seemed to possess a seraphic glow. Earnestly she besecched me to become a Christian, to love God with all my heart, and seek an entrance into Christ's fold, assuring me that only in so doing could I hope to obtain true happiness.

Two days previous to her death, her sweet bud of promise wilted and died; she did not mourn, for she felt it had but gone before to welcome her, a cherub in that land of bliss, where sin nor death enters. From this time she failed rapidly, and it became evident not many suns would rise and set ere her spirit would soar from earth away forever, to bask 'neath the ineffable glory of his countenance, who is the Lord of Hosts and worthy to be praised While sitting by her side the day previous to her death, she drew me to her, and kissing me affectionately said: "Mary, I have learned to love you dearly, but I shall soon leave you. I had hoped the one blessing you so desire would have been restored before my death, but this may not be; try and feel resigned to the dispensations of the Most High; and oh! promise to meet me in heaven."

She died loved and lamented by all who had known her. That same week her husband and father experienced religion, the sanctifying effects of their bereavement.

A few lines occurred to me which, humble though they be, I offer as affection's tribute to one whose gentleness and true worth still casts a halo of beauty around her memory:

Our loved one hath gone to her home in the skies,
Where suffering no entrance hath found,
Where sighs are all hushed in a gladsome surprise,
And the pure brow with glory is crowned.

She clasped to her bosom the dear little one
She so willingly gave to her God:
"My darling, we'll meet, when life's journey is done,
In yon beauteous, blissful abode."

Look up, stricken mourner, weep not thy dead,
Her memory lingereth yet;
Like the fragrance which flowers at evening shed,
It softens the pang of regret.

As sadly we lay her in the cold silent tomb,
And the heart throbs with fullness of grief,
We turn from the pall and the sepulchre's gloom
To the teachings of Christ for relief.

We see through the dimness of tears as they rise,
The crucified Saviour of men,
Who speaks, as he bends from his throne in the skies,
"Ye shall meet the departed again."

Thus it is ever. We love, and what we love, or bird or tree or flower or dear familiar friend, they vanish from our midst like the morning's early dew. Truly, "Man's days are as grass; as a flower of the field, so he flourisheth: for the wind passeth over it and it is gone; and the place thereof knoweth it no more." What a lesson should this teach us! Life's brevity and the unknown hereafter awaiting us beyond Death's shadowy portals. Day after day to the lonely graveyard we follow our loved, then return to the busy bustling world again, and, mingling in its anxious strife for gold or pleasure, forget the touchings of the voiceless lip or the eloquence of the form motionless in death.

. . . . . .

The morning of the twenty-second of February dawned bright and beautiful, fitting type of him whose natal day was to be commemorated by a virtue-loving people. But not in unison with the day were my feelings; a presentiment of ill hung over me. I can not define the indescribable dread with which the slightest sound fell on my ear. After breakfast I repaired to my cousin B.'s, to pass the day. It was nearly night, and nothing had occurred in answer to my nervous apprehensions. Suddenly the door-bell was rung violently; I nearly fainted, and yet I knew not why.

The new arrival was Cousin Maria, who had come to walk home with me, also informing me uncle Jacob was there, waiting to see me. Her voice in communicating this to me sounded strangely, and the manner of the rest of the family after we reached home struck me as unusual. I *felt* something had happened, and I anxiously awaited being informed as to what it might be.

Uncle Jacob spoke of the weather, and made an effort to introduce other topics of the day; in doing so he made an apparently casual and incidental reference to my father; inquiring if I would receive him kindly if he were to come to Baltimore. The truth flashed upon my mind in an instant. Springing to my feet and catching him by the arm, I exclaimed, " O uncle, has my father come?" to which he replied with a forced lightness of tone and manner: " I did not tell you he had."

He then told me to put on my bonnet and go

home with him, and I could ascertain for myself if he were there. When ready to start, he suggested I should take my brothers' and sister's likenesses with me. This made positive my impression that he was there.

The walk to Uncle's seemed much longer than it had ever done before, so anxious was I to *see*—nay, to meet my father, and once more hear his voice.

Aunt received us at the door, and as soon as I was in commenced removing my bonnet and shawl. Uncle Jacob led me to the sofa and said: "Mary, here is your long lost-father." In an instant I was clasped to his bosom. It was several minutes before he could command himself to speak. When the first intensity of feeling had subsided, he said: "Is this my little Mary?" He groaned aloud with very anguish, "Oh! can it be that you are blind forever; oh! no, we *must* get you cured!"

Every one in the room was weeping, but I could not shed a tear. At that moment my heart seemed turned to stone; my past trials and sufferings rose before me as vividly as though but a day or an hour had elapsed since

I endured them. Mrs. Ruthven's harsh, severe tones were again ringing in my ears. Again I was homeless and friendless. I could not realize it was my father sitting by me. He appeared a stranger to me.

Although fifty years of age, he could have well passed for thirty-five. His kind and affectionate manner soon won my heart, and I freely forgave him for what had appeared to me like neglect, during the long years that had intervened since he left me in the stage on my way to the home he had thought would be so pleasant and desirable.

When I would move about the room, he would earnestly watch me and refer sadly to my blindness. It made him very unhappy, and he would weep like a child. I showed him the likenesses, and he kissed them several times with much affection.

He told me he had lived in New-York most of the time since parting from us, and was married again, and that he had three children named after us—which proved he had remembered us, though far from him. He remained in Baltimore two months, then returned home to his family.

Spring had now opened. I was still under treatment for my eyes; they were no better, and it was thought best to dispense with the doctor's further services. Accordingly my bill was settled, and I was relieved the almost daily torture to which I had been subjected.

At this time I received an invitation to visit some relatives in Westminster. It proved a pleasant trip. I made many new friends. On my return Cousin William proposed I should go to New-York and try if any thing could be done to effect a restoration of my sight. Upon his advice, I wrote to Uncle Henry Deems, a resident there, asking him at a stated time to meet me. I started on the twenty-fifth of May. Cousin William could not go with me; but he placed me under charge of a lady travelling that way, a Mrs. Moreton; she was extremely kind and attentive.

We entered into a pleasant conversation, and I found she had known my father and mother. At Philadelphia we were joined by a lady and her little girl, ten years of age. She was quite agreeable, and while with us added much to the pleasure of our journey. On leaving the boat we were literally carried along by the crowd, and it was not until we were seated in the cars our new friend discovered she had lost her purse, containing about fifty dollars. She was much distressed, and so was her little daughter. At the first stopping-place the conductor telegraphed back, but nothing had been heard of the missing purse. A gentleman took his hat and going through the cars, lifted a collection for the lady. One man in his liberality put in a cent; but the gentleman immediately threw it out of the window, saying: "We want no coppers." When he had completed his noble errand, he returned and emptied the hat's contents into the lady's lap. She was too much affected to thank him, but her little girl did so more effectively than words could have done, by taking his hand and kissing it most passionately. Mrs. Moreton inquired his name, but he would only say: "I am from San Francisco."

The lady then gave Mrs. Moreton a sketch of her life. Her husband had died one year previous, and had unfortunately left his property in care of those who had defrauded her of it. To regain it if possible, had been her errand to

Baltimore; but the attempt had been unsuccessful, and she was now on her way home to Providence. A thousand-fold seemed magnified the generous deed of the noble Franciscan, when we learned the lost purse and its contents had been toiled for by one who had encountered such heavy misfortunes.

After we had taken the steamboat at Amboy, she went on deck to express her thanks to her friend in need, but he would not admit he deserved or desired any acknowledgment of what he had done; but said he purposed making a second collection on the boat — this the lady gratefully declined, as she already had recovered a larger amount than she had lost.

CHAPTER XVIII.

"GIRD up your heart with silent fortitude; suffering, yet hoping all things." HEMANS.

"FRIENDSHIP has a power
To soothe affliction in her darkest hour." H. K. WHITE.

"WHAT can we not endure,
When pains are lessened by the hope of cure?"
NABB'S MICROCOSMUS.

AFTER a few hours' ride, we landed at New-York. My uncle had been described to me before I left Baltimore; I asked Mrs. Moreton if a gentleman came into the cabin answering to this description, as I repeated it to her, would she speak to him for me. In a few minutes I heard her inquire of some one, "If he were looking for a blind lady?" He said he was, and she presented me to him. He received me with great cordiality, expressing thanks to Mrs. Moreton for her attention to me. She now bade me good-by, extending a pressing invitation to come and visit her, remaining just as long as I would feel inclined. The lady and her little girl also parted from me, kindly wishing me success.

Uncle then took me to his home; the affectionate interest there shown words can not utter The tenderest anxiety in my behalf was expressed, which I shall ever gratefully recollect.

The morning after my arrival, I went with Uncle Henry to Dr. Stephenson's Infirmary. I had been told he could decide, as soon as he had seen the patient, whether their sight could be restored; my suspense, consequently, was almost overwhelming. Having reached the place whither, it appeared to me, I had come to hear my fate pronounced, so excited was I, it seemed as though I should certainly faint. The doctor came in · observing how overwrought were my feelings, he very considerately forebore telling me how little probability there was I should ever see again.

While seated near us, one patient after another came to consult him relative to diseases of the eye. Some he would inform they could be cured, but others again, and by far the greater number, he would tell he could do nothing for them. Among these unfortunate ones there was a young woman who, upon learning her case was beyond human skill, sank back in her husband's arms, and I never can forget her groans of agony. Then the piercing screams of a man reached me; he was undergoing an operation in an adjoining room. My heart sank within me, when the doctor arose and taking me by the hand, said to my uncle: "I think we had better take her away from here, or she will be too unnerved to undergo an operation." We retired to a spacious parlor up-stairs, where the doctor left us alone. During his absence, Uncle tried to cheer me, begging me to exercise as much fortitude as I could. The doctor soon returned, accompanied by a Mrs. Sherwood, the lady of the house; she was about forty years of age, her once handsome face bore traces of care and sorrow. Her manner was winning and gentle, very motherly and soothing.

Uncle engaged board for me. My room was adjoining the parlor, most pleasantly situated. He then took leave of me, promising to call the next day. The doctor accompanied him, and Mrs. S., excusing herself, followed them, which left me, as I supposed, entirely alone. While musing over the events of the day, I heard a slight movement near me. I spoke but received no answer; this frightened me very much, but I arose to ascertain if possible what occasioned the sound I had heard as of some one moving, also a soft breathing I could distinguish. Now, gentle reader, what do you suppose had produced my alarm? Something very terrible, no doubt! say you. Well, it was a dear little girl about three years old; Nellie, she told me, was her name, and she had long curls which mamma said were pretty, very pretty, and that her eyes were blue like the sky. Sweet little prattler! how earnest was the prayer that went up from my heart that they might never be veiled by a misty shadow, shutting out forever the bright blue sky, whose cerulean hue had tinged them with beauty.

I twined my arms about her, and held her caressingly to me, when with tenderness beyond her years she asked: "Are you blind?" From Mrs. Sherwood, who had now returned, I learned Nellie's mamma was one of the boarders.

Mrs. S. conversed with me about many things, giving me stray snatches of her personal history. Her husband had died two years previous, and had left her with eight children, seven of which were sons. The tea-bell interrupted the continuance of our conversation. At the table I was introduced to the boarders, and to her two eldest sons, William and George Sherwood. George was quite talkative and agreeable, and we became pretty well acquainted. Tea over, he waited upon me to parlor, and spent the evening chatting with me. I felt I had gained another friend, for sincerity and kindness marked his every word.

The next week had been decided upon as the time when an operation upon my eyes should be performed. The day previous to the one of so great moment to me, Mrs. Sherwood came into the parlor accompanied by a very handsome lady and a little blind boy. Taking a seat near me, and appearing much affected, my hand held in hers, she said to me in earnest, sympathetic tones: "Are you blind?" On my assenting, she said: "So is my dear little boy!" Little Willie sprang into my lap, and throwing his arms caressingly around me, said in plaintive simplicity: "Did you stick a knife in your eye, too?"

Dr. Stephenson, entering at this time, examined my little friend's eyes, and pronounced the case a doubtful one as to relief. The distress of his mother at this intelligence was truly heart-rending. She had travelled from Minnesota, a distance of more than a thousand miles, alone, in order to avail herself of Dr. Stephenson's acknowledged skill; and to learn there in all probability could be but little done, was indeed a severe trial. The doctor, however, suggested she should remain awhile, and he would do all in his power. She said she would remain, provided I would allow her to share my apartment, to which I readily assented, thinking she would prove an agreeable companion.

The day following, Aunt and Uncle came over to be with me while my eyes were being operated upon. Dr. S. came in, accompanied by a number of other doctors. Their arrival so unnerved me that they thought best not to attempt the operation. Dr. S. suggested I should consult Dr. Wilkes before any thing further was done; accordingly the next morning, accompanied by Mrs. Biglow and little Willie, I called on this physician. He received us with great civility, but told me it would ruin my eyes to undergo an operation, that Nature was the best doctor He asked if there was an institution for the blind in Baltimore, and said he would advise me to return home and enter it as a pupil if there were one. He then examined Willie's eyes, but with the same hopeless result, of which he apprised Mrs. Biglow as kindly and delicately as he could. We then bade him good morning; Mrs. B. soon after left for Minnesota, for she was anxious to meet her husband and communicate to him how sadly fruitless had been her embassy. Ere we parted she gave me much good advice, and kneeling down offered up a prayer that the cup it had fallen to our lot to drink, might with resignation be quaffed, and that strength be awarded sufficient to endure our severe affliction.

At one o'clock we bade adieu to each other, promising to recollect kindly the intercourse we had held together, and cherish that friendship which had been formed under such mournful circumstances.

Contrary to Dr. W.'s advice, I determined again to make an effort to undergo an operation.

I did not feel that I could return to Baltimore satisfied without having done so. Saturday was appointed, and on that day Uncle was with me to sustain me as much as possible by his presence. One doctor after another came quietly into the room, thinking to do so without my knowledge. I told them they could not frighten me to-day, so they need not be so very quiet and cautious. Seated upon an ottoman, they all surrounded me, Dr. Stephenson in front, as he was to perform the operation, and tried to cheer me by talking gayly. He said: "I was right good-looking, and all I wanted was my sight." I told him "not to flatter me, or I should lose all confidence in him." This conversation occasioned great laughter. Then all were very silent, for Dr. S. commenced the exercise of his skill. It lasted about twenty minutes, during which period I fainted four times. After he had finished he laid aside the instrument, saying: "My dear child, I have done all in my power, we must leave the rest to God." He also said: "I had borne up wonderfully, and would make a good soldier." Uncle was much affected. I was placed in a dark room to remain until the bandage over my eyes could be removed. When the time had expired, I found to my great joy I could see distinctly. How unutterable was my delight at this discovery; but I was doomed to disappointment. As my eyes healed, vision departed again; and the world, the faces of those I loved, was henceforth to be to me a universal blank.

George Sherwood proved a firm and steadfast friend. He was indeed a noble young man, towards his mother tender and respectful, and endeavoring to sustain an almost paternal relation towards his younger brothers. He whiled away many evenings reading to me, and his selections were always very beautiful.

I never loved a stranger as dearly as I did Mrs. Sherwood, and she expressed herself similarly of myself, our tastes seemed so congenial. She was ever studying something for my enjoyment. George's health failing, the doctor ordered him to the country; when he had gone I felt lonely, the evening reading had been such a delightful pastime.

Dr. S. could do no more for me, and I concluded to return home. I regretted parting with Mrs. Sherwood and her family, but

> "There is no union here of hearts,
> That hath not here an end;"

so bidding them farewell and asking not to be forgotten, I left for home. Dr. S. said he would have given half he was worth to have cured me, but, as this had been beyond his skill, he could but wish me many friends and success in whatever I might at any future time undertake. He was very kind and gentlemanly.

Uncle placed me in a lady's care travelling to Baltimore, and having bid him and his dear family good-by, I was once again a bird of passage; still in the dark, for though I had gone in search of light, it had been denied, and it now became my duty to submit unrepiningly to His decrees who suffereth not even a sparrow to fall to the ground unnoticed, who is mindful of what is best for the weakest of his creatures.

CHAPTER XIX.

"THESE eyes—
Bereft of light, their seeing half forgot;
Nor to the idle orbs doth sight appear
Of sun, or moon, or star throughout the year,
Of man or woman: Yet I argue not
Against Heaven's hand or will, nor bate a jot
Of heart or hope; but still bear up and steer
Right onward." MILTON.

"AND thou shalt touch for thyself, the golden sceptre of Religion." TUPPER.

. . . .

"So, that blessed train passed by me; but the vision was sealed upon my soul;
How beautiful their feet, who follow in that train."
TUPPER.

MRS. SIMONS was a very pleasant lady, and we chatted the time away quite agreeably. We stopped at Philadelphia, and most of the passengers went to the hotel to dine. A lady desiring to do so, left in my charge a small basket filled with gold, until she should return and claim it. A little while after, she came back into the car and took the basket from me, saying:

"I placed great confidence in your honor in leaving my treasure in your care." "Not at all," said I; "You knew I could not see to run away with it, no matter what my disposition might have been." These remarks amused the passengers; they seemed fully to appreciate my inability to appropriate the lady's gold by running away with it.

We reached Baltimore in the evening; home once more. Truly, "there's no place like home." After my return I spent several weeks at Uncle Jacob's. Being now fully satisfied there was no hope that my sight would be restored, I resolved to submit to my lot unmurmuringly, indeed with what of cheerfulness I could, believing it would but make "the day more dark and dreary," wasting it in idle repinings. My friends were anxious I should enter the Institution for the Blind, as had previously been advised. Cousin William was at this time in Europe, and it was thought best not to delay matters until his return. So anxious was I to become a pupil that I made every personal effort to attain so desirable an end. I found unshrinking perseverance necessary to bring it about.

Aided by Professor Loughery, Superintendent of the Institution, admission was obtained. The day I left Aunt's, again to make my home with strangers, is one thronged with various memories—emotions of pain as well as pleasure. I was sad at leaving home, and hopeful as to what I might accomplish in self-improvement during my stay in the Institution.

Cousin Mattie accompanied me. On entering we were met by Mr. Loughery, one of the most perfect gentlemen I have ever known. He also was blind, therefore could deeply sympathize with those to whom had fallen a similar affliction. The welcome he gave was very cordial, hoping I would be happy and contented while in the Institution. He then excused himself and left the room. A few moments and a young lady came to me, introducing herself as Miss Moran, the assistant teacher. I was much pleased with her manner, so graceful and lady-like. Cousin Mattie bade me good-by, promising to visit me the next week. Miss M. conducted me to the sitting-room.

School being now dismissed, the young ladies, pupils in the Institution, entered. At this time, there were only three female and five male pupils. Upon being introduced they greeted me as though I had been an old acquaintance. This is the usual manner of the blind; they are never strangers to each other, a common sympathy seems to link them wherever they meet. They are shut out from the external world around them, and feel that a mysterious tie makes them kindred to any who have been denied, like them, the power to *see* as well as *feel* that God is very great, as all his handiworks proclaim.

Miss Moran gave a lesson in the art of sewing, in which instruction I participated. Mary Vernon was the most advanced pupil; she could dimly discern the outline of figure, also could distinguish light from dark. How great blessing to be able to do even this. She was a very lovely girl in disposition and manner. The sewing hour passed, Miss M. led me through the house and grounds, and though October with its presaging voices echoed amid the trees, the garden was still beautiful, neither the fruit nor flowers had as yet all departed. We next went to the music-room, where we found Prof.

Loughery performing on the piano; he entertained us for some time. We were joined by Anna Buckler and Mary Poteet, who came to conduct me to be introduced to Miss Alcorn, the matron. She received me very pleasantly, saying: "She was happy to have another added to their little band."

The bell rang for tea. The arrangements and regulations of the Institution seemed very strange to me at first, I had been so indulged at Aunt's; however, I soon accommodated myself to them.

The next morning I went into school. I do not think I shall ever forget my first attempt to read. I thought it impossible I ever should learn, but my motto was, "Where there's a will, there's a way;" and I determined if application would enable me to surmount the difficulty it should be overcome. So with my various other studies, knowing "what had been done could be done again," I resolved to make every possible effort, hoping in the end to acquire knowledge which I might devote to practical purposes, as well as enjoy, as the rich reward for what of toil and labor, the effo. ight have cost me.

. . . . . .

As I have before said, Cousin Sarah urged me to promise to meet her in Heaven. Latterly this subject had occupied seriously my thoughts. I was in the habit of attending the Lutheran Church, in Monument street. During my visit to New-York, a new pastor had been appointed, which I regretted, thinking it impossible any other could acceptably fill Mr. Lilly, the former pastor's place. But I decided, at least to hear the stranger, and then form my opinion as to his merits. Accordingly, I went to church Sabbath morning and heard Dr. McCron deliver as powerful a sermon as I had ever listened to. It had great effect upon me. I returned home deeply convinced of my sinfulness of heart. Feeling somewhat prostrated from my excited state of mind, I lay upon the sofa and fell asleep, when I dreamed I had died, and in an instant was at the gate of heaven. I was no longer blind. At a silver desk covered with writing materials, there sat a strange-looking man. He turned and looked at me in a manner so searching, it made me shudder—then asked in a tone of voice that sounded like thunder in my ear: "Do you wish to enter the gate?" On my telling him "I did," he said: "Have you a ticket from God?" This query made me wretched. During this conversation the gate had repeatedly opened to admit those who on earth had secured a ticket entitling them to an entrance.

The light streamed forth in such crystal brilliance, I was forced to cover my eyes to shield them; and the loud hosannas of those who heard the welcome words, "Come in: of such is the kingdom of heaven," almost deafened me. My agony was intense—Heaven's gate closed against me—no entrance there for me; like the foolish virgins my lamp had not been found trimmed and burning. From this painful imagining I was aroused by a well-known voice,

happy indeed, to learn 'twas but a dream, "if dreams they be which have so strong a power o'er heart and brain." I resolved to heed the warning given, and secure ere too late, those graces and Christian virtues, which, united to a pure heart, and firm faith in Him who died to

redeem a lost and ruined world, would entitle me to a home with those who alone see God.

I sought an acquaintance with Dr. McCron, and under his prayers and teachings became a member of the visible Church the May following. The day of my confirmation seemed the happiest I had ever known. As I knelt at the altar I felt as though a heavy burthen had been lifted from me, that had hitherto been weighing me down to the very earth. I can not express the happiness I experienced; I felt at peace with all the world. The voices of my friends sounded like sweetest music in my ears; I thought I never could sorrow again. Since that to me eventful period, Dr. McCron has been as a father, ministering pious counsel and holy teachings. I can at all times freely unburthen my heart to him, and am ever sure not to be turned empty away. Tender sympathy and hopeful words seem ever to spring up in response, to even the faintest whisper of sorrow or regret. May his labors be abundantly acknowledged of the Lord, and the seed he has sown broad-cast in the land, produce a harvest which shall redound in glory to the Most High God.

CHAPTER XX.

"Roses bloom, and then they wither;
Cheeks are bright, then fade and die;
Shapes of light are wafted hither,
Then like visions hurry by." PERCIVAL.

"Let there be no noise made, my gentle friends,
Unless some dull and favorable hand
Will whisper music to my weary spirit."
SHAKSPEARE.

"The over-curious are not over wise." MASSINGER.

"You cram these words into mine ear, against
The stomach of my sense." SHAKSPEARE.

I HAD now been in the Institution six months, and had made greater progress in my studies than I had at first anticipated. The Board of Managers were extremely kind and attentive to us. Two of them were particular favorites with us — Messrs. J. Trust and B. F. Newcomer. Whenever they visited the Institution they would come to our sitting-room, and laugh and joke, greatly to our amusement and entertainment. Mr. T. frequently sent out for ices for us, which we deemed a great treat coming from him.

The pupils all loved and respected Mr. Loughery, and although he was blind, there was not one who would take the least advantage of him. Their love almost amounted to worship; indeed, he was idolized by many, and one and all took pleasure in refraining from aught that he might disapprove. I never have known more perfect government than he maintained. Very intelligent and of affable manners, he won not only the hearts of all his pupils, but also of every one with whom he met. No sacrifice seemed too great for him to make, if it in any way contributed to our gratification or enjoyment.

To our great sorrow, during the spring he was taken ill, and confined to his bed three months. This was a season of painful suspense to us, for it was not thought he would recover. The dawn of each day brought the fearful anxiety lest it should be his last. As time sped, however, he partially recovered, and we were most thankful to have him once more restored to us.

During his illness every instrument of music was hushed and silent, for no one felt any inclination to indulge in this recreation and he so ill. While upon his sick-bed he composed the following beautiful and touching lines, which were set to music by Professor Magruder, who also is blind.

MY MOTHER'S PARTING TEAR.*

"When far away from home and friends,
A slave to fortune's will,
My heart oft turns to other days,
And her who loves me still.
I see the last fond look she gave,
Of mingled hope and fear,
And still I see as though 'twere now,
My mother's parting tear.

"When tossed upon a weary bed,
Of sickness and of pain,
No friend to cool my fevered brow,
I see her face again.
When friendship seems to be a name,
And all the world is drear,
I know there's one who loves me still,
I see her parting tear.

"Sweet visions of my early home,
Steal nightly through my sleep,
And fancy soars on dreamy wings,
High o'er each mountain steep.
Soon may I see my good old home,
And childhood's friends so dear;
I long to glad my mother's heart,
And wipe away her tear."

* Published by George Willig, Charles street, Baltimore, and by his kind permission here inserted.

Miss Alcorn left at this time, and her place as matron was supplied by Mrs. Sawyer. Professor Loughery had been our teacher in music, but he was now relieved of this duty by Prof. Magruder, whom we soon learned to cherish as a dear friend, each day revealing some new trait to be admired. Being himself blind, he could bear patiently with us, also could from this fact the better appreciate the obstacles under which we labored in acquiring facility in this most delightful accomplishment.

Vacation had now arrived. I could not have realized how attached I should become to those with whom I had been thrown so short a time. It seemed like one harmonious loving family, and I felt loth to leave them for even a brief space. The autumn following, our public concerts held in the hall of the Institution, began. It was at first a great trial to me to perform in public, but gradually I became accustomed to it.

Remarks made by strangers would sometimes greatly amuse us. On the regular visiting-day there was generally a fund of after-merriment laid by at the expense of a few anxious inquirers after information as to what they supposed were the peculiarities of the blind. They appeared to regard us as a race distinct from themselves. Some would ask: "If we closed our eyes when we slept as did seeing persons?" Others would inquire: "Do you not have great difficulty in finding the way to your mouth when you eat?" Some would even go so far as to express a desire to see for themselves *how* we ate. There were those who seemed to consider us frightful objects, of whom they were afraid; and again, I have known persons to put their mouths to our ears and scream as though they thought we were deaf as well as blind. They would also stand close beside us and pass remarks upon us, as though they thought we were as unthinking and unfeeling as might be a breathing statue. I have known them to say aloud and immediately by our side, "We were the ugliest people they had ever seen," or "that we were pretty and interesting." These and similar comments were constantly being made in our presence as though they thought because we were blind we had also been deprived of reason, and were but moving automata, walking stocks of wood or stone!

There is very generally, I think, a false impression as to the life of the blind. Many suppose they spend much of their time mourning over their one great affliction; this is quite a mistaken idea. They are as cheerful as seeing persons; and indeed, take an equal number of either, and it would, I am sure, be found the *majority* of those contented with their lot, and disposed to take the events of life resignedly, would be those who saw not external things, save as their fancy might depict, and who would give to all the sunny or the shady hue with which their spirit might imbue scenes and persons with whom they are thrown.

There are many who are of opinion it is impossible for the blind to be educated; this, however, is erroneous. During my connection with the Institution, I think I have acquired quite as much practical information as I could possibly have done had I had my sight. The educated blind in their own home are as useful and industrious as are those who have not been deprived of their sight. They are handy and ingenious. Generally speaking, they are cheerful and happy in disposition, social in their feelings, cherishing the most delicate sympathy for each other. Their conversation is less of earthly realizations than of heavenly anticipations. They talk with delight of that land where night cometh not, and where no sorrow entereth.

Persons are but faintly appreciative of the sensitiveness of the blind to acts of kindness. Though trifling in themselves, little acts or little words breathing tenderness will endear a stranger to them at once. Nor are they aware how keenly alive these unfortunate ones are to harshness or neglect. A tone will affect them more deeply than a volume of severe expressions would those whose pathway has been unshadowed.

Though the enjoyment of earth's manifold beauties has been denied them, though veiled from them is the delicate blush of early morn, or the fading sunset glow, yet there are chords in their souls that vibrate as do the strings of the Æolian to the gentlest zephyr, making sweet though plaintive melody.

Because God has seen fit in his infinite wisdom to hide from us the face of friends, he has none the less implanted within us kindred sympathies, a yearning to love and be loved again. Sweet Friendship, with her fond endearments, is as necessary to the happiness of the blind as to those who can recall glances of fond affection expressed by

> "Tones and looks that dart
> An instant sunshine through the heart,
> As if the soul that minute caught
> Some treasure it through life had sought."

CHAPTER XXI

"The banquet waits our presence." Brown.

. . . . .

"Then all was jollity,
Till life fled from us like a pleasant dream." Rowe

"Around her shone
The light of love, the purity of grace." Byron.

"Her gentle spirit
Commits itself to yours to be directed
As from her lord, her governor, her king."
Shakspeare.

The Maryland Institution for the Blind, opened in December, 1854, with two pupils, Miss Mary Vernon and Samuel B. Stewart. It was established through the energy and perseverance of Professor Loughery, who had been educated in the Philadelphia Institution for the Blind; also was a graduate of the University of Pennsylvania. It had been his intention while pursuing his studies, at some future day to establish in Maryland an Institution for the Blind, similar to the one in Philadelphia; to Mr. Magruder, a fellow-pupil, he frequently expressed himself as being resolved to make every effort to accomplish so desirable an end. He on one occasion remarked to Mr. M.: "Jim, when I have founded such an Institution, you shall be my music-teacher." How fully was this plan fulfilled! A few years elapsed, an Institution was established, Mr. Loughery appointed its Superintendent, and Mr. Magruder Professor of Music.

Mr. McHenry, the President of the Board of Managers, has always shown effective interest in the welfare of the undertaking. He had an addition to the house built, thereby rendering it more commodious; also contributed a furnace heating every room; independent of these accessories to our comfort, he with several other gentlemen of the Board have made liberal donations. Mr. Trust presented a beautiful organ, which afforded the pupils much pleasure, as they were anxious to learn to perform upon this instrument. Dr. Fisher provided a piano, besides liberal donations. This gentleman also evinces great interest in our improvement.

During January, Prof. Loughery's health

very perceptibly failed, so much so it was thought advisable to appoint some one to assist him in his labors. Dr. McKenney came as Superintendent. In the spring, Mrs. Sawyer left us, and her post was supplied by Miss R. Bond. There is one other inmate of the Institution to whom I would make a passing allusion. I refer to "Biddy," our faithful waiting-maid; she was the first attendant employed, and proved herself at all times a noble-hearted woman. No matter how busily engaged, upon hearing any one of us express a wish, she would lay every thing aside and render the desired assistance.

My friends were desirous I should make one other effort in attempting to find a cure for my eyes, and proposed I should try the effect of electricity; accordingly I was placed under Dr. Massey for treatment, hoping possibly he might do something for me. Every morning, Cousin Georgie H. was in the habit of calling to accompany me to the doctor's; these morning walks were of great benefit to my health, and the application of electricity strengthened my nerves, but my vision was not improved.

Enjoying Cousin Georgie's society, how many happy hours have I spent in her father's, Uncle B.'s family. She indeed, in my estimation, is almost a perfect being, amiable and good, and endowed with a sweet melodious voice. She sang most beautifully, and while sitting listening to her, I would forget I had sorrows, and would think earth a very paradise. Uncle and aunt always welcomed me with a parent's embrace. Oh! how thankful I should be in having so many and such kind friends; and deeply grateful I feel when, in retrospecting the past, those days are recalled when I was a lonely, motherless, friendless wanderer. God has indeed raised up many to care for and feel an interest in me, and I often outpour my heart in thankfulness to him, for his loving-kindness and tender mercy towards me. I deeply sympathize with those who have fallen under a like misfortune with myself, and who have found but few to sympathize with them, and cheer with sunny word or kindly act their darkened way. Miss Schofield, a Quaker lady whom I met at the Institution, and who was in the habit of attending our weekly public concerts, expressed a desire to contribute in some way to my happiness and comfort. I informed her how fortunate I was in having many friends, but named to her some of my schoolmates who had very few, and hoped she would remember them kindly. She promised to do all that lay in her power for them, and she has religiously kept that promise, having been a staunch and unfailing friend to the Institution and its beneficiaries ever since that time.

Vacation during the very warm summer weather was now approaching, and we were to be examined in our various studies before the Board of Managers; the anticipation of which caused us great nervous excitement and anxiety, it being the first examination into the proficiency of the pupils. The day at last arrived, and for our beloved teacher's sake, we resolved to exert ourselves to our utmost ability. The second day of examination, Mr. Trust invited us out to the back-porch, where was a table set with refreshments. We were much delighted with this attention, and some remarked: "This is just like Mr. Trust." After having enjoyed the repast, we one and all heartily thanked him, to which he responded: "All the thanks he desired was to see us enjoy it."

The May previous, a Fair had been held at the Institution in behalf of the pupils. It was superintended by Mr. Yearly, in which noble effort he was assisted by several young ladies. Mr. Y. is very kind, generous man, and exerted himself greatly, in having the Fair yield as much as possible. Strangers who attended were very kind to us, and tendered us many delicate attentions.

Vacation arrived, we were compelled to part, though only for a brief season, with our beloved teachers. This really seemed as severe a trial as though the separation were to be one of unnumbered years instead of a few swiftly fleeting weeks.

I spent the two months' release from duty very pleasantly among my relatives and friends, and in the autumn returned to my studies with renewed ardor and increased desire to improve the numerous advantages with which I was blessed. Professor Loughery's health had much improved, and there was but one circumstance which cast a shadow over our reünion, and that was the intelligence our dear teacher, Miss Moran, was about to leave us; this information grieved us very much; she had been so gentle, so good and kind, we thought no one else could fill her place. But she was to be married, and we were forced to yield the happiness of her sweet presence to another who could prefer a stronger claim. The evening previous to her departure Cousin William gave us a large party, to which were invited the pupils and officers of the Institution, besides other of my most intimate friends, among whom was Dr. McCron, who most agreeably entertained all present with his lively and engaging conversational powers. We went at an early hour, and shortly after having assembled, we all repaired to the supper-room, where we found oysters dressed in every variety of manner awaiting our enjoyment. Previous to taking our seats, Dr. McCron made a short but appropriate prayer, after which we did ample justice to the good things spread out before us.

Having adjourned to the parlor, we played on the piano, sang and conversed in the most lively manner, Professors Loughery and Magruder taking an active and prominent part. Every countenance save one was beaming with plea sure; our dear teacher seemed sad, it was the last evening she was to be with us, and we were all deeply attached to her. The next day she was to leave those who for three years had been constantly with her.

A second time we repaired to the supper-room, where was a table set in the most elegant manner, covered with an abundance of confectionery and ices—indeed, every thing that could be mentioned. After spending another hour very pleasantly together, we returned home, every one expressing themselves as having passed a most charming and agreeable evening. No unimportant personage at this most delightful entertainment was Cousin Samuel H., who is a great favorite with all at the Institution; so attentive and agreeable was he, that scarce a wish could be conceived, much less expressed, before he was close at hand to gratify it. His many kindnesses to me I can not enumerate, and can only desire that friends he may make may prove as genial and as faithful as he has ever been.

Cousin William had not married again; Cousin Mary, a most estimable lady, taking charge of his household and family arrangements. I have ever found in her a true friend; gentle in manner, sensitive as the delicate aspen leaf, her whole life has proved her

> "A perfect woman nobly planned,
> To warn, to comfort, and command;
> And yet a spirit still and bright,
> With something of an angel light."

That the happiness she has conferred, return upon her own heart fourfold, is my earnest prayer.

The day Miss Moran left us, was one of mournful interest; we were all so much affected we could scarce attend to our morning recitations. In the afternoon she bade us adieu, promising often to visit us.

The following Monday, a lady to supply her place was expected; we all wondered what sort of person she would be. Some thought she could not possibly be as desirable as had been our former friend; others said they *knew* she would have a harsh voice, and be very disagreeable, and that she would be some old person who would not allow any merriment or pleasure. At last Monday came; and with it arrived the new teacher. Contrary to all surmises, she was a sweet youthful girl—a musical voice and merry laugh, were not by any means by us deemed her least desirable attractions. She soon won the affections of the pupils, and proved herself fully competent to her office, though very young. Our necessities and little pleasures seemed her constant and unceasing study. We shall ever remember her as an angel that flitted athwart our way, bringing sunlight to chase the shadow. Wherever in after-life her path may tend, she will bear with her warm aspirations for her welfare from the hearts of those whose way, though dark, she has oft illumed by cheering word and radiant smile.

CHAPTER XXII.

"And every where,
Low voices with the ministering hand
Hung round the sick." Tennyson.

"O Death! O Beyond!
Thou art sweet, thou art strange!"
E. Barrett Browning.

"When sorrows come, they come not single spies."
. . . .
"One woe doth tread upon another's heel,
So fast they follow." Shakspeare.

About a year previous to our change in teachers, a young lady from the Philadelphia Institution for the Blind, paid us a visit, remaining with us, however, only a week, during which time she instructed us in bead-work. Of this we had availed ourselves with much earnestness, and had learned to make a number of little fancy articles. The happy Christmas time approaching, we determined to apply the proceeds of our labor in this way towards making Mr. Loughery, our beloved teacher and friend, some gift as a token of the deep affection we entertained for him. The amount realized from the sale of our bead-work had been, from time to time during the year, carefully hoarded. A meeting was called, and the pupils expressed their wishes as to its appropriation, and a gold chain and key were decided upon. All our little plans had been executed without his knowledge, and an evening appointed to consummate the surprise. It at last arrived. Prayers over, Dr. McKenney rose and said to Prof. Loughery: "He would be a principal actor in a little scene about to take place." Prof. L. arose, and Miss McGinley presented in a graceful manner our offering, accompanied by a neat and touching address. For several minutes he was too much affected to speak. His emotions subsiding, he replied: "I fully appreciate this, as it was purchased by your first earnings. I prize it the more deeply coming from those for whom and in whom I feel such a deep interest, and shall preserve it as long as I ——" His feelings quite overcame him, he could say no more, therefore hurriedly left the room. Every one present was affected to tears.

In wearing the chain and key, persons observing it would remark how pretty it was—he would reïterate to them how dearly he prized and with what pleasure he wore it. A memento of the love of those knit to him by no ordinary friendship.

The Legislature were now in session, and the last of January we were going to Annapolis, accompanied by the officers of the Institution, and the Board of Directors. Our object was to give a concert and exhibition, thereby endeavoring to excite an interest in our behalf, and secure an appropriation for the purpose of improving and enlarging the Institution. Our errand was deserving encouragement, as certain changes, which money alone could accomplish, were greatly needed. During our stay in Annapolis we were the guests of Mr. Tidings, who was extremely kind and attentive. The exhibition was the first we had attempted beyond the walls of the Institution, yet we gave, as far as we could learn, general satisfaction. We returned to Baltimore delighted with our trip.

The following month Prof. L. was again in Annapolis, pursuant of the effort we had made, and endeavoring to bring as much influence to bear in our behalf as he could. The Legislators expressed themselves as having been astonished at our proficiency and delighted with our musical performances, yet closed their session without granting our petition. So great was Prof. L.'s disappointment, he returned home ill. Dr. Haynel was called in, and pronounced his disease congestion of the brain. We had greatly missed our cherished friend during his brief absence from us, and to have him return so ill was indeed a severe distress. While feeling intensely anxious as to his recovery, I was summoned to attend the funeral of my beloved Uncle B. He had been complaining about a year, but we little thought his death so near. The last time I was with him in life, I told him before I met him again, I hoped he would be better. He silently embraced me for a few moments, then said: "Yes, my dear child, I shall be better when we meet again." Ere again I sought his side he was a cold, inanimate corpse; his sufferings ended, earth had forever passed away, and heaven had become his everlasting home. As I knelt by the sofa, whereon lay his loved form so cold and still, and pressed my hand on his chilled brow, I thought of all his benefits and tendernesses to me. I felt I had lost one of my best friends, I followed in imagination, his ransomed spirit, to realms of bliss where angelic choristers hymn ever songs of praise, and longed to loose this mortal coil, and like him be forever free. How prayed I that so would my Heavenly Father guide and protect me, I might once again meet those who had gone before, who had tracked the upper stars and passed into Eternal Glory.

We laid him in the silent tomb and left there the form so dear; but he felt not its gloom, heard not the wailing voices of those who mourned, for his spirit was afar off with "just men made perfect." And as we call to mind his many virtues:

"His memory, like some holy light,
Kept alive in our hearts will improve them;
For worth shall look fairer and truth more bright,
When we think how he lived but to love them."

During the summer previous, Prof. L. had had several hemorrhages, and was now rapidly wasting away from that fatal disease, consumption. Dr. Haynel did all human skill could do to bring about his recovery, but in vain. Dr. Johnson was consulted, the physician of the Institution, but unavailingly. Three others were also consulted, but with the same hopeless result. Nothing more could be done for him than already had been done.

On learning this, our grief was indescribable, for we loved him as dearly as though he were a brother. His physicians advised he should go to the country, as change of air might benefit him some little. His brother came to take him home to that mother whose parting tear he so plaintively expressed—and for whom there was now in store bitter sorrow and many tears.

His parents were residents of Pennsylvaina. A few days after his brother's arrival he was prepared to go. Never shall I forget the morning of his departure. All the inmates of the Institution assembled in his room to bid him a long, a last farewell. One by one in silence bade him good-by forever; oh! the agony of emotions that swelled our hearts. We could not speak, words would not come, they were powerless in this hour of separation. Tears abundant copious tears, took their place, and eloquently told the wealth of affection garnered in our hearts for him who was now leaving us. He too sobbed like a child, for severe as was the trial to us, equally seemed it so to him. He had been counsellor, brother, friend, and we had drank rich draughts of knowledge from lips that ere long would be hushed in death.

He was lifted from his couch and borne to the carriage, and as it rolled away our grief knew no bounds. It seemed as though we had parted from our last, best friend. Just at this time Mr. Newcomer entered and cheeringly said to us: "Come, girls, you have dwelt long enough upon the dark side, the other is all bright and beautiful. Should Mr. L. never return to you, you can go to him. If called to pass Jordan's narrow stream, your loss, though great, will be his infinite and everlasting gain." "I know it is hard for you to part from him, but God, who is too wise to err and too good to be unkind, hath so ordained; therefore you must try and be resigned; to his will. In your grief you have the consolation that you have ever obeyed his counsels, that his instructions have ever fallen on willing and ready hearts to follow the way he should guide. Then do not murmur or repine at a dispensation rendered by our Heavenly Father. He saw fit to rob him of his manly strength and beauty, and we can but submit."

Mr. N. had always been much beloved by our little band, and these words of consolation found us willing listeners; they calmed our troubled spirits, and made him dearer to us than he had ever been before.

The friends who were kind and attentive to our beloved teacher during his illness, will ever be remembered by us with deep emotions of thankfulness. Miss Bond never wearied waiting upon him. Many a delicate attention from her reached his couch of suffering soothingly; she is indeed a noble-hearted woman. I too, can recall her tender solicitude by a sick-bed, for she has oft made less weary unto me, the nours of languishing and pain.

CHAPTER XXIII.

"Soon may this fluttering spark of vital flame
Forsake its languid melancholy frame!
Soon may these eyes their trembling lustre close,
Welcome the dreamless night of long repose."
Campbell.

"And they who before were strangers
Became straightway as friends to each other."
Longfellow.

"There is a divinity that shapes our ends,
Rough-hew them as we will." Shakspeare.

"So fare thee well! and may the indulgent gods
. . . . . . grant thee every wish
Thy soul can form! Once more, farewell!"

After Mr. Loughery's departure we were very lonely, and it was thought best to dispel this gloom by passing our evenings out from the Institution among our friends. With Miss Bond I was kindly invited to Mr. Thomas Armstrong's. He had lately married a very agreeable and interesting lady, formerly resident of Harford. A few days previous to this visit, I had been so fortunate as to become acquainted with Mrs. Lee, Mrs. Armstrong's mother. We were mutually pleased; she evinced deep interest in my welfare, also in that of the Institution. Mr. Armstrong is a religious and generous-hearted man, has great sympathy for the afflicted.

Before going to tea we joined in singing a beautiful hymn of praise, and Mr. A. kneeling led us in prayer. With my hand clasped in good Mrs. Lee's, listening to that fervent prayer, I felt as though in very truth the Holy Spirit hovered nigh, and I arose with my heart strengthened to do his will and love him supremely. This calm, genial evening will ever be recalled, as some bright oasis with purling brook and grassy breast is remembered by the traveller who has tracked the desert sands. Such hours cast a glow of joy over our hearts, and we learn

"Friendship is not alone a name,
A charm that lulls to sleep;
A shade that follows wealth or fame,
And leaves the wretch to weep."

Mrs. Lee returned home shortly after, and I have not since met her; yet happy am I to have learned she has not forgotten me, though many miles lay between us; frequently I have received kind messages of love from her. May her declining days be peaceful and happy, irradiated by the light of His countenance who is the joy of her heart and her portion forever.

Dr. Wilson, (Mrs. Lee's brother,) upon visiting our Institution, expressed great interest and sympathy in our behalf. Though I met him but a fleeting hour, I found him social, genial, and most agreeable as a friend.

We were very anxious until we received intelligence of Mr. Loughery's safe arrival home. We still deeply felt his absence from us; two of our number, Thomas Maxwell and William Davis, were almost inconsolable. They had watched and tended him day and night during his illness, devoting themselves to him with the most unremitting attention.

The night before he bade them adieu, he gave them much good advice, also made each a present of a penknife, which they still possess, and value very highly.

Thomas Maxwell had been thinking seriously on the subject of religion during his teacher's illness, and, I am happy to say, has since been converted, and has become a consistent member of the Presbyterian Church.

Among the mementos of my dear departed friend, I cherish a few lines penned for my album. I give them to the reader, sanctified as they are to me by tender recollections and loved associations.

THE QUEEN OF FLOWERS.

"One clear summer night through the garden I strayed,
With thoughts sad and pensive, alone;
The pale moon was soaring in beauty above,
And gilding the earth as she shone.
The bright stars were studding the heavens like gems,
And watching the weary at rest;
And mild, gentle zephyrs in fond, playful mirth,
The sweet sleeping flowers caressed.

"The roses were dreaming of beauty at morn,
As they slept in their own shady bowers,
And close by their side stood a figure divine,
The beautiful Queen of the Flowers.
She gazed on them fondly, e'en Venus ne'er looked
More charming, more lovely than she,
Sweet innocence played on the dimples that came,
And her smile was a heaven for me.

"Aurora arose in her pure robe of light,
And chased the dull shadows away;
The roses awoke from their beautiful dreams,
To welcome the bright orb of day.
The fair Queen of Flowers, no longer remained,
She left them, I thought, with a sigh,
And dew-drops, like mirrors, reflected the love
That beamed as she smiled a good-by."

The Trustees of the Institution, finding Mr. L.'s health not likely to be regained, engaged Professor H. H. Bruning to instruct us. He proved very competent, and we made progress in our various studies. He endeared himself to us by the sympathy he expressed for us in the loss of our former preceptor; said he once had a teacher whom he loved and respected as a parent, and that having had to mourn his death, he could feel for us in our separation from one whom we had cherished so fondly.

We heard occasionally from Mr. L., but unwelcome the intelligence, for every letter but confirmed the melancholy fact that he was rapidly declining, and that ere many moons had waned, his earthly pilgrimage would have ended, his sands of life quite run out.

One afternoon, while assembled in our parlor, Biddy entered, holding a letter sealed in black. I can not describe the feeling that came over me; in an instant every voice was hushed, and a deathlike stillness reigned. Miss McGinley broke the seal, yet spoke no word. The suspense became painful, and we implored her to let us know the worst. In a husky whisper she replied: "Girls, he is gone!" Every heart was bowed in grief—these words had sped like barbed arrows. Sobs and groans were heard through every part of the building. Such sorrow I never wish to witness again. Each inmate seemed to feel they had lost their best friend. We could scarce realize that a few months previous he had been so well, cheerful, and happy, and was now beneath the burial sod, the cold turf above him.

His words and actions arose to our memory, and were lovingly treasured by us. And well might we recall the past when he was with us and of us, for even in his dying moments we were near unto him. Just before his spirit took its heavenward flight, even when delirium was raging high, he talked of our stricken band; imagined himself again in the school-room, or whiling the hours away in discoursing sweet melodies to us. But he has gone, and we are left to sigh and weep that earth knoweth him no more.

He would sometimes say, could he have his two homes together, he should get well faster. But he was not to be restored to health; the fiat had gone forth, and it became our duty to say, "Thy will be done, O Lord!" and strive to subdue the sorrow surging in our hearts. Sweet friend,

"Light be the turf of thy tomb!
May its verdure like emeralds be;
There should not be the shadow of gloom,
In aught that reminds us of thee.

"Young flowers and an evergreen tree,
May spring from the spot of thy rest;
But nor cypress nor yew let there be,
For why should we mourn for the blest?"

In two weeks after Mr. Loughery's death, one of our pupils, Summerfield Bassford, a young man of fine promise, aged twenty years, exchanged this world for a brighter and far happier one. Death had entered our band and stolen from it two shining marks, transplanting them to bloom in heaven.

Again vacation was drawing near. I was glad to obtain release from duty, for the sorrow of the last two months had greatly impaired my health, and I sadly needed surcease from toil.

Cousin Charles Harriman kindly invited me to pass my vacation with his family. This invitation I readily availed myself of, for I felt sure it would recruit both my health and spirits. Accordingly the day-school closed; I left for Westminster. You may, gentle reader, fancy my pleasure in again greeting my cousin's family, not having seen them for two years. They tried every means to divert my thoughts from the sad past, and at the close of my hours of idleness I returned to my duties, feeling much improved physically, and more cheerful than when I had laid them aside to seek the invigorating influence of country air and healthful exercise.

During my absence Dr. McKenney had resigned the superintendence of the Institution, and the Board of Directors were about supplying his place. As may be supposed, the inmates were very solicitous as to who might be elected to the post. Much of their comfort and improvement depended upon this decision.

Would it be some one who would sympathize with them as Mr. Loughery had done? Or would he deem his office not one of tender friendship, and loving, Christian counsel, but as that of mentor, whose word was a law irrevocable?

At length the day arrived upon which the important decision was to be made. After the adjournment of the Board, Mr. McHenry, its worthy President, came and informed us Mr. Charles Keener had been elected. Though a stranger to us all, yet the appointment pleased; we felt he would prove all we could possibly desire.

We were now daily expecting his arrival. It was quite as much a matter of debate among the pupils as had been that of other expected officers. As in previous instances, his voice was anticipated as likely to be indicative of his disposition towards us. We did not fancy it would be harsh or severe, but a sort of internal consciousness seemed to inform us it would be kind and gentle. Yet prepossessed as we were disposed to be in the stranger's favor, still we thought he could not possibly be just like our loved and lamented friend and teacher.

Four weeks elapsed ere Mr. K. came; when one morning all assembled in the school-room to receive the new arrival, which was to us of so much moment. How eagerly we listened for the first sound his lips should utter; it was to be the index of our future. He spoke a few pleasant words of greeting, and the magic tone of kindness was not wanting. A smile flitted over each countenance. He would prove as we had thought he would. Mr. K. ever referred in a kind and sympathetic manner to our bereavement in the death of Professor L., saying he felt for us and with us in losing so dear a friend. This appreciation of our sorrow made him at once seem very near to us, and from each heart went up a prayer that his life be long spared, that he may tread the paths of usefulness, dispensing light and cheer to all whose sun is darkened here below.

And now, gentle reader, the simple story of my life is told. You mayhap have met but little to win upon your fancy, yet these pages are the heart-history of one whose way has indeed been fraught with vicissitude. Gleams of sunlight have shone forth, even when the hour was darkest, bidding my sad heart cheer, no day so dark but hath a bright to-morrow. If you have paused to shed a tear over any line or one emotion of sympathy has swelled your bosom in behalf of the lonely, friendless wanderer, then have you called forth gratitude from the heart of one keenly alive to what of joy may be her portion.

While wending your onward footsteps to the grave's shadowy portals, may no cloud obscure the light of your earthly horizon, and when with its icy chill shall steal death's hand over the heart once responsive to the ennobling emotions, pity, friendship, love, may an angel bear to the home of the blessed your ransomed soul, to dwell forever with the Lord.

www.ingramcontent.com/pod-product-compliance
Lightning Source LLC
LaVergne TN
LVHW010742120826
845150LV00009B/1403

* 9 7 8 1 4 2 5 5 1 7 1 7 5 *